Becoming 1% Better

Copyright ©2025 by Natalie Saar

All rights reserved. No part of this book may be used or reproduced in any manner whatsoever without written permission except in the case of brief quotations embodied in critical articles.

While every effort has been made to ensure the accuracy of the information in this book, the author and publisher assume no responsibility for errors, inaccuracies, or omissions. Readers are encouraged to verify information and consult with experts as needed.

This book is intended for informational and educational purposes only and should not be taken as professional advice. The author and publisher disclaim any liability for any actions taken or not taken based on the information presented.

The views and opinions expressed in this book are those of the author and do not necessarily reflect the views of any organization or institution with which the author is affiliated.

The author and publisher do not guarantee any particular results or outcomes from using the information in this book. Readers are responsible for their own actions and decisions.

This edition is self-published by the author.

ISBN 978-1-7378835-3-1

Dedication

For my siblings. Family is ever.

Becoming 1% Better

100 simple changes to improve your life 1% at a time

By Natalie Saar

Table of Contents

1. Acceptance (p12)
2. Adventure (p15)
3. Algorithms (p19)
4. Alignment (p23)
5. Anger (p28)
6. Anxiety (p33)
7. Authenticity (p37)
8. Balance (p41)
9. Beginners (p45)
10. Behavior (p48)
11. Bodies (p52)
12. Boundaries (p56)
13. Breath (p60)
14. Chaos (p63)
15. Codependence (p67)
16. Commitment (p70)
17. Community (p73)
18. Comparison (p78)
19. Confidence (p83)
20. Conflict (p86)
21. Connection (p90)
22. Consistency (p94)
23. Creativity (p99)
24. Curiosity (p103)
25. Daydreaming (p107)
26. Decisions (p111)

27. Disappointment (p114)
28. Discipline (p120)
29. Drive (p123)
30. Emotions (p128)
31. Expectations (p132)
32. Failure (p136)
33. Fear (p140)
34. Forgiveness (p143)
35. Fun (p147)
36. Gentleness (p152)
37. Goals (p156)
38. Gratitude (p160)
39. Grief (p164)
40. Growth (p170)
41. Guilt (p174)
42. Habits (p179)
43. Healing (p182)
44. Idling (p185)
45. Imposter (p188)
46. Increase (p192)
47. Increments (p195)
48. Inner child (p199)
49. Introspection (p202)
50. Kindness (p205)
51. Laughter (p208)
52. Learning (p211)
53. Leisure (p215)
54. Lessons (p220)

55. Mind-reading (p224)
56. Mistakes (p228)
57. Money (p232)
58. Motivation (p235)
59. Movement (p238)
60. Negativity (p242)
61. Newness (p246)
62. Opinions (p250)
63. Patience (p255)
64. Perfection (p259)
65. Perspective (p263)
66. Presence (p267)
67. Pride (p271)
68. Problems (p274)
69. Purpose (p279)
70. Reality (p284)
71. Relax (p288)
72. Rejection (p292)
73. Resilience (p297)
74. Resistance (p301)
75. Risks (p304)
76. Routine (p308)
77. Sadness (p312)
78. Seasons (p317)
79. Self (p321)
80. Self-compassion (p326)
81. Self-love (p329)
82. Self-sabotage (p333)

83. Service (p337)
84. Shame v341)
85. Sleep (p345)
86. Specialness (p351)
87. Stillness (p355)
88. Storytelling (p359)
89. Surrender (p363)
90. Time (p366)
91. Today (p371)
92. Trauma 375)
93. Trust (p379)
94. Unplug (p383
95. Urgency (p388)
96. Vibrations (p392)
97. Vulnerability (p396)
98. Whimsy (p399)
99. Wins (p402)
100. Words (p405)

Introduction

Ever since I was a super shy kid and picked up "How to Win Friends and Influence People," I've been captivated by the idea that we can make small tweaks to the way we move through the world that benefit both us and those around us. Over time, I implemented many of the techniques I learned from that book and others, and have now successfully fooled everyone I meet into thinking I'm an extrovert.

In addition to being a self-improvement enthusiast, the sports fan in me also loves a good set of data. So, I started to figure out a way to track my own personal improvement. I'd note how many days a week I was contributing to various areas of my life (friends, family, hobbies, health, work, school, projects, etc.) and was able to highlight where I lacked focus. As you can imagine, this became a little demoralizing because there are only so many hours in a day, and I was always lacking in one of these buckets. Then around a decade ago, I stumbled upon the idea of being 1% better every day. Now *that* was something I could handle.

Aiming to be 1% better every day freed me in two ways. First, it supported my curiosity about how to pursue becoming a better version of myself, and second, it made that pursuit achievable and empowering instead of overwhelming.

Then about two years ago, I decided to start sharing these ideas in a Substack of the same name as this book. It received such positive feedback that I thought it would be a good idea to add more themes and compile it into a resource that could reach more people. That is the book you're holding in your hands right now.

My hope is that whether you're a busy parent, professional, or just someone who is feeling a little off, you'll find one tool in here to help you feel like a better version of yourself. If you're looking to add a little more levity in your day or want to find gentle ways to become more disciplined, there's something here for you.

I do want to call out that there are huge bodies of research about every one of these subjects. While I do include some specific scientific references, these chapters are meant to be short, actionable insights that you can read in about five minutes, which (if you'll indulge the data-lover in me) is less than 1% of your day (it is 0.3472% of your day, if you were curious). There are some truly wonderful, easy-to-digest books that dive into many of these topics, so if there's one that you find particularly helpful or intriguing, follow that itch and see where it leads you.

You may also notice some repeating themes in these chapters and that's intentional. It often takes our brains a few times to receive new information, intake it, and then act on it. But each section is still structured to focus on one specific topic.

Also, none of this is meant to supplement medical advice. If you need help, please seek that out. Therapy, including tele-therapy, has become much more popular and accessible in recent years, so please seek out those resources if you need support.

Bettering ourselves requires change, and as you'll learn in this book, our brains are constantly battling against change because it can be scary. So give yourself a ton of credit for even being interested in this book in the first place.

And now, without further adieu, let's get started.

Acceptance

What is and what could be

Sometimes when people hear the word "acceptance" they think of it as giving up or not making things better than they are now. But that couldn't be further from the truth. Acceptance is simply that: accepting that a certain circumstance exists in its current form. But you always have the power to change circumstances, even if it's simply changing your mentality.

For example, maybe you were passed over for a promotion or didn't get a job you really wanted, or worse, maybe you got a dream job only to find out that it's a nightmare. Do you beat yourself up about it? No way! You just accept your current circumstances and make a plan to move on.

Whenever we fight accepting something as it is, that creates resistance, and resistance is always heavier to bear than non-resistance.

Maybe you are dealing with a difficult person, or a person you're close with has become challenging for some reason. You don't need to stress about "fixing" them, you just need to accept them as they are and move forward. Maybe moving forward means you have less contact or maybe it means your relationship shifts to more meaningful forms of communication.

And what would it look like if you accepted *yourself* just as you are? People are constantly looking for ways to change themselves whether it be on the inside or the outside. They think that they aren't enough just as they are, and that's not true. We can all continue working on ourselves every day, aiming to be 1% better, but that doesn't mean you shouldn't love yourself just as you are right now.

If a child is learning to read but can't yet read large words, that doesn't mean you criticize and give up on the child. You understand that they're learning at their own pace and you work with them to help them get stronger.

What if you did that for yourself? What if you thought about that one thing you are hardest on yourself about and said, "You know what, I'm working on this, and maybe it's taking a little longer than I'd like or than it takes for other people, but I accept myself as I am right now, and I'm going to support myself while I keep trying."

How would that feel?

If you're on a diet, you don't give up because you had a donut in the break room at work, or if you're starting a new hobby, you don't quit because your finished product doesn't look like someone else's who has been doing it for decades. You just acknowledge that you'll get there and keep it moving.

Today, can you be 1% better by accepting yourself and your circumstances exactly as they are right now. Release judgement for how you may have gotten here and give yourself credit for the fact that you're trying, and you're loving yourself in the process.

Reflection

Adventure

Every day is a new day

I laughed as I wrote the headline for this chapter. Audibly laughed. Because you'd be hard pressed to find someone who would associate me with "adventure." When I think of adventure I think of Bear Grylls, Amelia Earhart, and others. I don't think of… me.

But that's where I'm wrong.

I heard a clip from Dr. Joe Dispenza the other day that struck me. The distillation was this: Approach each day like a new adventure.

We all hear the alarm every morning. Maybe your alarm is a phone alarm, a child crying, an actual rooster that your neighbor bought and you *hate* them for it. Whatever it is, something alerts you to the day, and you begin processing. What you need to do, where you'll go, what needs to be executed during the day.

But hear me out… what if you didn't?

What if you woke up and felt the same way you did as a kid when you were going to Disneyland, or on a field trip, or whatever made you feel alive when you were young.

What if you — an adult with a job — woke up thinking, "I can't WAIT to explore the adventure of today! I don't know what will happen, but it'll be great!"

It sounds… exhausting. But it also sounds… exciting!

I don't know about you, but I want to wake up and be *excited*! Excited about what? Nothing! Everything! Who knows! I don't. You don't. As much as we think we know what will happen that day, we don't!

So, the day after I heard that clip from Dr. Joe, I tried it out. I heard the alarm. My brain fell into a pattern until I stopped it: Wait! This is the day where I don't know what will happen! It's an adventure! Unexpected things will happen!

You know what happened? Nothing. I sat at my desk for two hours before another teammate showed up at the office. But right around every corner I mused... maybe magic will happen. And again... it didn't.

Maybe this sounds depressing but I promise, I had the coolest day at work. Every email was an invitation to adventure. Even if the adventure didn't pan out. I had such a good day that the next morning I did the same thing. And the next.

I thought I'd get disappointed after a while... but I didn't. Because the world is filled with wonder if you *expect* it to be. Maybe not overt excitement, but the wonder never ceased. And what is life without wonder?

So maybe you try this and you don't find *"adventure."* Maybe no one approaches you with a life changing proposition to sail the seven seas in search of a long lost buried treasure. But the treasure isn't the goal (duh). It's the journey.

Every day you have the chance to search for adventure and treasure, even if it isn't the conventional, tangible kind.

Try to be 1% more curious and approach the day like an exciting adventure. I've got to tell ya, even waking up in that mindset made me feel at least 1% better.

Reflection

Algorithms

You direct your life's algorithms

We hear the word "algorithms" in relation to social media, but believe it or not, it also applies to your social and personal life. The same way your clicks, swipes, pauses, and interactions influence what content you'll be shown online, your daily choices influence what will show up in real life.

Think of your life choices as a self-directed algorithm. Whatever you choose to do signals to your brain that it was the "right" choice and helps ingrain that pattern. But sometimes there are no "right" choices. If you've had a long day, it isn't the "right" or "wrong" choice to pick up dinner on the way home. It was simply your choice. And once you do it, it becomes easier to do it the next time, then the next. You're choosing to tell your brain that this is a preferred process.

Now, draw this out into other areas of your life.

How do you talk to yourself? The words you say begin a process that will become easier to follow time after time. If you speak kindly to yourself, you'll be likely to do that more often and show yourself more compassion.

Who do you surround yourself with? You collect people you want around you as you go through life. You're self-selecting your social algorithm. So, surround yourself with people who reflect the qualities you value and want to call into your life.

Think of a time when someone or something you were thinking about just SHOWS UP. Isn't it like when you say something out loud and you magically get ads for it? Chances are that in thinking about that subject, you subconsciously took steps to bring yourself closer to the opportunity to interact with it.

This is sometimes called the Law of Attraction and while the Law of Attraction is still considered pseudoscience, there are some logical findings you can take away from the theory.

If you want to paint a masterpiece, you start by getting some paint and studying works you want to emulate.

If you want to read a book, you start by buying or borrowing one.

If you want to play an instrument, you start with one note.

In other words, you attract the outcome you want with your actions. And your actions influence your brain's processing system. So, over time, your self-directed algorithm aligns you closer to the outcomes of your actions.

Just as social media platforms curate your experiential algorithm for what you express that you're interested in, your brain — which is also a type of computer — alters your lived experience based on your actions.

How can you become 1% better at influencing and controlling your own self-directed algorithms in a positive way? Can you speak kindly to yourself? Can you be the one to plan social outings instead of waiting for an invite? Can you start by admitting out loud what it is that you want in life and thinking about how to move towards it? Even taking a mental step in the right direction is a step. Always remember you are in charge of your own algorithms and how you choose to experience life.

Reflection

Alignment

Pay attention to the wobbles in life

Have you ever driven a car with bad alignment on the freeway? If you have, you know the wobbly, bouncy experience it offers. If you haven't, just picture driving a bumper car on the open road, not going quite the way you wanted and swerving around. When you feel this in your car, you know something is wrong.

Life is similar. We know within us what we should be doing. I'm not talking about "right or wrong," but rather our actions. Intuitively, we know what our purpose is on Earth, sometimes it just takes a little longer for our conscious mind to understand it. So, how can we better sync up with that purpose, especially if we don't know what it is?

One tactic I've found helpful is alignment. When I'm doing something and get the feeling that it's not right anymore, I stop and consider the situation before moving forward. It's important to separate the feeling of something being hard or difficult with not "being right". Our brains can make us think that new, hard things aren't right because our brains don't like anything new. But that doesn't mean it's not right.

If you find a house that on paper is perfect, but there's just something feeling off, you wouldn't buy it, would you? If you go somewhere and get a feeling that you should leave, you do, right? If you meet someone and get a strange feeling from them, chances are you'll find a way to politely excuse yourself.

We live in a state of being where not only is the world itself busy, but our minds are busy. There are so many everyday things to do (chores, work, life maintenance) and also so many fun things to do. Unless you make a conscious effort, chances are good that you don't spend a lot of time tuning into your intuition to seek the decision that's right for *you* in each of these moments. If you don't do that, then you're just going with the flow, bumper car-ing around.

Food is the best example I can give for this because what each of our bodies need is unique. I am a vegetarian and my body truly feels ill if I eat meat, but I have friends who conversely feel sick without eating red meat every now and then. We all need different things at different times. If I don't workout, I often don't feel super hungry during the day. So when I get the feeling to have a little snack while I stare into the fridge trying to figure out what my real snack will be, I have to stop and ask myself, "Am I actually hungry or does my brain just think I need to eat food right now?" Once I started approaching snacking like that, it changed my relationship with food, aligning it to a path that was effortlessly more healthy for my body.

Think about what you do during the day. Have you felt those little mental tugs saying, "I should go on a quick walk," "I need to stretch," "I'm not enjoying this show that everyone else loves." Pay attention to those and start heeding the cues. Soon, you'll find that you are feeling better and have more enjoyment in your life.

I made a conscious effort to do this as much as possible one week to test out the theory. I saw a huge and almost immediate improvement in my mental health. I always tell myself to go outside in the afternoon and make it productive by walking. But I don't actually like walking. I think a lot of runners can relate to this, but walking just feels so… slow. So, I decided to start doing what I actually wanted to do, which was go to the beach and just sit for a while. The days I heeded that call, I felt so happy, chill, and inspired for the rest of the day, things I almost never feel after going on a walk. When I'm working on a writing project, if it just isn't feeling right, I step away from it for a bit instead of powering through with my original plan. I have yet to find a time when this wasn't the right decision.

Learning to seek alignment in our lives can actually be a fun little experiment that also helps you stay grounded in the present. We make 33,000-35,000 decisions every day. That's about one decision every 2.5 seconds. What if you stopped and thought through some of those decisions from the framework of alignment? Remember, it's not always your initial conscious thought that is your intuition.

Can you make 1% more of your decisions by choosing alignment? When you are sitting on the couch and think, "I should go outside but I also really should relax," let your intuition guide you to the decision that is aligned with your ideal version of yourself. When you think about how you'd like your life to be, ask yourself if the decision you're making will help you get closer, further, or neutral from the way you want to feel? Neutral is also fine, but try to avoid choosing the option that will get you further. You have at least 33,000 opportunities every day to align with your ideal self, whatever that means to you.

Reflection

Anger

You hold all the power

Anger knows how to push my buttons and I typically know how to keep it at bay. But sometimes anger gets the best of me. I thought I understood anger until my 20s when I once got so angry that I couldn't see for a second or two. I used to think it was a dramatic myth that people got blackout angry but it's true. If you've ever stood up too quickly and your vision gets spotty, it's like that.

In fact, it's got a name: Vasovagal syncope. It's "a sudden drop in heart rate and blood pressure leading to fainting, often in reaction to a stressful trigger."[1] But beyond that, science has struggled to fully understand anger. It's based on a fight, flight, or freeze response and sometimes it overwhelms our nervous system if it becomes too strong. Besides that, it's a very individual feeling.

So, we know that we have this strong response that our body perceives as a threat without much conscious thought. What do we do with that information?

The good news is that anger can actually be a very powerful tool for us if we learn how to harness it. I recently heard cyclist Lance Armstrong in an interview where he talked about an incident at a bar. While he was waiting for his rideshare, some guys started

---

[1] Grossman, Shamai A. "Syncope." *StatPearls [Internet].*, U.S. National Library of Medicine, 12 June 2023, www.ncbi.nlm.nih.gov/books/NBK442006/.

yelling and ridiculing him over his past scandals. He was understandably upset when his car finally arrived and said he felt like he needed to take action. But he obviously wasn't going to go back and fight them. He decided the "action" was to call the bar and buy a round for the same guys who were verbally attacking him. He asked the bartender to make sure they knew it was from him and to tell them, "I get it."

I found that to be such a powerful example of how to quickly process anger and turn it into a healing moment for both him and those guys, to validate the pain he caused them, to take responsibility for his past, and to also fulfill his angry need to "take action."

We don't have control over when anger hits us, but we do have control over how we respond to it. I think the most fascinating part of anger is how and why we all experience it differently. One person getting cut off in traffic is no big deal, but to another it'll send them into a fit of road rage. What upsets you may not even phase the next person. That's okay. Remember, anger isn't "one size fits all" and will look different to everyone. You're not wrong if you're the only one upset about a situation. There's just something within your subconscious that deems the situation a threat, and is therefore sounding the "anger alarm."

What can we do? Well, consider how powerful anger is. It's sudden and sometimes overwhelming. It can strike out of the blue. That's quite the force, but it can be reckoned with. Imagine what you could do with that anger if you gave it a little space then harnessed it for good for yourself or others.

What if you went out for a run when you felt angry and turned it into a healthy activity? What if you played a song you love and did a little solo karaoke session to move the energy out of your body? What if you stopped, took a few deep breaths, and physically signaled to your nervous system that everything is okay and you're not in trouble?

One time, I was stopped at a red light and someone walking in the crosswalk banged on the hood of my car for no reason at all, then kept on walking. I stopped and said, "God, may the energy they receive today match what they put out." I've continued doing that ever since then. It helps me stop, consciously acknowledge the anger I feel, acknowledge that what they did felt wrong, and then give it up to a higher power. I also like that it isn't wishing ill on them, it's simply acknowledging that what we put out into the universe, we also receive.

Another thing I like to do when I feel angry after seeing upsetting stories in the news is donate to a cause that's relevant to how I feel about the situation. It's a small thing, but like Lance Armstrong's story, it's still an action that helps me move the anger and frustration out of my body.

If you feel anger rising up, how can you let it go 1% more? Can you take a walk? Take a deep breath? Simply acknowledge in the moment that you're feeling angry and name the emotion?

What are some other methods you personally use to deal with anger?

Reflection

Anxiety

Making friends with anxiety

When I first learned about anxiety in my 20s, I remember being devastated to find out that there is no cure, that not only was this a feeling we all had to live with, but a healthy amount of anxiety actually helps us survive and thrive. Anxiety is a biological response that keeps us alive. It's a good thing. Or at least it can be.

Unfortunately, the way our world functions, we're constantly hurtling into the future, ever diverging our connection with our bodies in favor of a connection with our conscious, thinking brain.

With anxiety, we need it to alert us to dangerous situations, but we also need to learn to have a healthy relationship with it.[2]

Every now and then, I experience what's called a globus sensation. My throat feels like it has a huge lump in it, and I have a difficult and sometimes painful experience when I swallow, and it can last for days. In reality, there's nothing in my throat at all. It's physiologically normal. This imaginary throat lump is triggered by my anxiety, and it presents itself during times of high stress.

The globus sensation was what drove me to learn more about anxiety in the first place. I had a stressful job with a manager who was actively and transparently trying to get me fired. Every

---

[2] Price, John S. "Evolutionary Aspects of Anxiety Disorders." *Dialogues in Clinical Neuroscience*, U.S. National Library of Medicine, Sept. 2003, pmc.ncbi.nlm.nih.gov/articles/PMC3181631/.

submission was a triggering event. I'd heard of anxiety, but I didn't know anything about it. While reading NBA coach Phil Jackson's book "Eleven Rings: The Soul of Success," I started to peel back the layers of how truly tightly wound I was.[3]

It inspired me to read the life changing book "Zen mind, Beginner mind," I joined a local yoga studio, which helped lead me down the most meaningful path of my life. I'm happy to report that after two months of non-stop globus sensation, each day I experienced more and more relief during the day where I was able to swallow without pain until it finally went away.

In a weird way, I'm glad that my body gives me a physical sign that I'm very anxious and stressed, otherwise I might never slow down and reconnect with what's really going on. Understanding and establishing your personal healthy level of anxiety is so important to your overall wellbeing.

Take some time today to stop and listen to your body. What is it telling you? Are your shoulders tense? Are you thirsty? Are you hungry? Are you at peace, and if so, what activities brought you to that peaceful place? It's amazing what our bodies will tell us if we'll be still, quiet, and listen.

Anxiety is something that's important to me, so at the risk of this being a longer chapter, I'll share one other method that I've found super helpful in my own life: make friends with your anxiety. When you are meditating, or just zoning out (on a walk, in the shower, in

---

[3] Jackson, Phil, and Hugh Delehanty. *Eleven Rings: The Soul of Success*. Penguin Press, 2014.

bed, wherever) and your anxiety pops up, acknowledge it. Don't try to push it away. Simply say to yourself, "Hello Anxiety, here's your seat at the table." And just let it be.

As with almost anything in life, the more we actively resist something, the heavier it feels. Think of a wall. If you casually lean up against it, it just feels like a nice place to rest. But if you turn towards the wall and try to push it away, then it's going to feel immovable. And I get it, sometimes life is just very heavy and stressful and you can feel out of control. So try to control *yourself* as much as you can by accepting what is and letting go of the rest.

The more we can learn to accept things as they are, to "make friends" with the circumstances, the better off we'll be in both the long- and short-run.

The next time you're experiencing anxiety, pause for a moment. Acknowledge and accept that anxiety is present, see where you feel it in you body, observe what triggered the anxiety in the first place, and then finally, don't judge it. If you can become aware of even 1% more of the factors that make you anxious, over time, you'll learn how to deal with them in a healthy way when they come up.

Reflection

Authenticity

What's authentic is what's right

Authenticity has always been a tough concept for me to wrap my head around. As a person who was raised in the church, went to a very small K-12 school, and who was always around business people, I always acted like I was *expected* to, not like I *wanted* to. And I got so good at it that it wasn't until I was in high school when I realized I did not know how to tell a joke. I had no concept of what my own sense of humor was. I laughed when it was appropriate and re-told the same jokes I'd heard in these respective settings. So, I started practicing how to add my own original jokes into conversations… but I still didn't actually understand what I thought was funny. As you can imagine, it didn't go well at first and I was often met with blank stares.

But I didn't let it stop me. I was determined to figure out what *my* sense of humor was and what I thought was funny. It took several embarrassing years, but eventually, I got there. Now, ironically, to some people I am "the funny friend" just by being and saying what feels right to me. In fact, the last thing my grandma said to me before she passed was that I bring laughter everywhere I go and to never let the laughter die.

When it comes to authenticity, there's a lot of trying things out before we figure out who we really are, and we need to give ourselves the space to experiment. Throughout our lives, our well-intentioned caregivers put us into different environments that mold us. Maybe you were forced to play a musical instrument but actually hated it, or you were forced to play sports when your more authentic self is not super competitive. There's any amount of combinations of conditioning that you may have gone through that shaped you into the person you are now.

There's an entire industry and branch of the "self-help" world that aims to teach people to be their authentic self, so I won't go into that here, but instead would tell you to seek out people who have done extensive work in this field if you want to learn more.

What I *do* want to share with you is how you can start finding out who you authentically are and what's meant for you *today* without needing to read or listen to anything else. I once met with a career coach and we discussed some issues I was having at the time. I am a Type A personality, and I find it disrespectful of people's time to mince words; those are two hallmarks of how I am wired. I told her, the only way I can continue on this project is to fundamentally change or hide who I am because the others don't work the same as me. I'm fine hiding away who I am if it gets the job done, but that was antithetical to the authenticity work we'd been doing in these sessions.

After about 40 minutes of us exploring the situation, she finally said to me, "What if this feels hard because it's not what's meant for you? You know this is a project *for now* not *forever* and that's why it feels hard because it's just another stop on your journey."

That blew my mind. Sometimes things feel hard because they are not what's meant for us. The situation creates its own resistance to indicate to us, "Hi, you may not feel great about this, and that's okay because something better is coming. You're just here for the moment."

In your own life, think about what's feeling inauthentic right now, or where are you being forced to present an inauthentic version of yourself? Now think about where you want to go in life. What are your personal goals? Could it be that this crisis of authenticity is actually a guidepost for you, to show that even though you're here right now, this isn't for you?

Okay, there were a lot of personal anecdotes in this chapter, but as a person who craves examples, it felt like if ever there was a time to let them fly, it's the one on authenticity.

If you've never thought about who you authentically are, like Teenage Natalie didn't know what her sense of humor was, spend some time exploring the way you think and act. Are you a certain way because it feels *right* or just because it was modeled and expected of you?

If parts of your life feel hard right now, examine if they're hard because you're acting in an inauthentic way or if they just don't line up with what's authentically you, and then can you give yourself grace to know it might just be a rest stop on the way to what's really meant for you. Try to uncover just 1% more of who you really are and what feels right.

Reflection

Balance

It looks different for everyone

I love lists. Sometimes I even make lists of the lists I need to make. It helps me organize my brain. It also helps me see what's on my plate for the day and figure out how I can balance it all.

Over the years, I've made (truly) thousands of variations of "to do" lists and project lists. But the one that revolutionized the way I view how I use my time is the one where I tried to balance my entire life.

At the risk of sounding like a madwoman, I'll explain. I color coded every task according to what its purpose was. Red was work-related, orange was creative projects, yellow was self-care, green was doing things to nurture my relationships, blue was life maintenance (chores, errands, etc.). I'd add or remove categories, I'd change the color coding, whatever needed to be done to evaluate how to find balance. But no matter how many variations I tried, it became brutally clear that every week looked different from the next and none of them were what I'd call "balanced." It was impossible to find a consistent steady balance because LIFE HAPPENS. And when life happens, our plans change.

The good news is that the takeaway here isn't that balance doesn't exist. It's that balance is different for everyone on every day.

Your body is a perfect example of this. In yoga asana practice, you treat each side of your body like a completely different part of your body. Just because you balance well on your left doesn't mean you'll balance well on your right. And just because you could do something yesterday doesn't mean it's accessible to you today.

Balance changes every day. Which is good news because it means you can find a balance whenever!

Of course, there are times when life gets crazy and you truly can't find your center, and it feels like you're just going, going all of the time. When that happens and you sense it happening, STOP. Stop what you're doing, take three deep breaths, inhaling through the nose and audibly sighing out of your mouth. This "cyclic breath" will help you calm down almost instantly, which gives you space to organize your next move.[4] If you're feeling out of control, make that next move something to help yourself. It may be as small as taking a drink of water or maybe something longer like taking a walk outside. Help yourself restore a sense of centeredness, even if your tasks for the day don't feel balanced. You can still aim to feel balanced within.

And if you're reading this and thinking, "Wow, I have never considered balance. I have no clue what balance might look like." Don't worry, there are tools to help that don't require a meticulous color coded list. Start by simply observing your day and consider

---

[4] Leggett, Hadley. "'cyclic Sighing' Can Help Breathe Away Anxiety." *Scope | Stanford Medicine*, Stanford University School of Medicine , 22 Mar. 2024, scopeblog.stanford.edu/2023/02/09/cyclic-sighing-can-help-breathe-away-anxiety/.

where your time is going instead of just blindly moving through the motions. From there, you should have a sense of what did and didn't feel right. What do you want to have more of in your day and what do you want to have less of? Can you find a way to shift things around and seek that balance?

There's a popular phrase, "We all have the same 24 hours in the day" but the truth is that those 24 hours look different for us all. Be 1% better by not judging yourself based on the balance *someone else* looks like they have in their 24 hours — or even by what *your* 24 hours looked like just yesterday! Just take each day as it comes and look for balance in the moments. It'll build up to a feeling of balance overall.

Reflection

Beginners

Adopt a "beginner's mind"

I've been practicing meditation since 2012 when I picked up the book "Zen Mind, Beginner's Mind"[5] and it changed my life. The general premise of "beginner's mind" is to approach everything with curiosity, like a beginner. Like you've never seen or encountered the thing or situation before.

Having this mindset helps us stay present. And staying present is what helps us stay more peaceful and at ease. If we get caught up in the past, we churn up all kinds of emotions like sadness, anger, regret. If we get caught up planning for the future, we may feel anxious, anticipatory, or start making a list of things that need to get done.

However, if we approach each moment with a beginner's mind, it changes the perspective.

Imagine you're in traffic. No one likes sitting in traffic. You're thinking about what happened that day at work and what you need to do when you get home. You're doing anything but being in the present moment because in that moment you are quite literally stuck and powerless to the stuckness.

Now try to imagine traffic with a beginner's mind and be curious. Look at all of the cars around you, and the people inside them. You're all dealing with the same scenario (traffic) at the same time

---

[5] Suzuki, Shunryū, et al. *Zen Mind, Beginner's Mind*. Shambhala, 2020.

(now), and that's kind of cool to think about. You're having a shared experience with complete strangers you'll never meet. And what about the radio? How crazy is it that the sound you're listening to is just traveling through the air?! There are so many things to observe and be curious about.

One necessary clarification: the point of a beginner's mind is not to simply occupy your mind with things in the present, but rather to observe them. See what's going on around you and take note.

When we approach life with a beginner's mind, it helps us find more fullness in each moment.

It's easy to say, "be present," but it's much harder to *do*. Try to find 1% more opportunities where instead of assuming you know what will happen, you know what to do, etc., approach it with a beginner's mind.

Reflection

Behavior

What are our learned behaviors?

Are there some things you do or habits you have that every now and then make you stop and wonder why you do them? They don't feel right to you, but you do them anyway, and you're not sure why. These are called learned behaviors.

From the moment we're born, we have behaviors that are innate to us and others that are learned. An example of an innate behavior is something like a baby grabbing a finger. No one had to teach the baby to hold the finger when it's placed in its palm, it just already knew to do that. A learned behavior is something that we are taught to do, possibly because of our environment. (NOTE: There's a huge body of work on this subject if you want to dig into it. I'm talking about entire college degrees, devoted to the topic, so at the risk of going down a rabbit hole, I'll keep it simple here.)

While our innate behaviors feel natural to us, some of our learned behaviors may not, and we carry them with us our entire lives unless we make a conscious effort to identify them and change the ones that don't feel right. For example, some people are taught that it's not okay to show emotion, when in fact, showing emotion is very healthy for us.

In my family, we didn't have a bedtime as long as we didn't hassle our mom when she woke us up in the morning, and we often ate dinner pretty late in the evening. As I grew up, I learned that this wasn't the case in many other households and these were behaviors I learned because of my environment. While I am still very much a night owl at heart, daily obligations now require me to unlearn staying up until all hours of the night so that I can get a good night's sleep and be up early in the morning.

Learned behaviors can also be stories we tell ourselves. I've had to work on rewiring how I think about fitness. As a teen and through college, I went to the gym nearly every day, working a different muscle group each day for about an hour. Now, I don't always have an hour each day, so I need to constantly remind myself that a 20 minute workout is still "worth it" if that's all I have time for.

Think about some behaviors you have that don't necessarily resonate with you. Maybe you were taught that you need to be 15 minutes early to every appointment, or you were told to speak a certain way around certain people. Is there something your family does that you later learned in life is unique to you? And do these behaviors feel authentic or do they feel like you're forcing something?

If a learned behavior feels forced or unnatural, then stop and consider it for a minute. Does it *genuinely* feel unnatural or does it just feel unnatural because you're not used to it? Sometimes when we're changing our beliefs and the way we move through the world, change can feel "wrong" simply because it isn't what you're used to. Our brains prefer the safety of doing what we know, so you may feel resistance when you're first making a change, but in the end, you'll be supporting a more authentic version of yourself.

Can you be conscious of just 1% more of your learned behaviors and ask yourself if you think it's truly a behavior that suits you or if it's just something you were taught along the way? If it doesn't feel right, can you give yourself permission to start trying to unlearn it or tweak it in a way that feels better to you?

Reflection

Bodies

Bodies are perfect

I've been thinking about bodies a lot lately and how much pressure we put on them. Every body is different in countless ways. If a nose is shaped a certain way, its owner may be more prone to sinus infections, migraines, and other ailments. If someone's foot bones are aligned a particular way, they're more prone to bunions. True story: my ears are two different shapes. I learned this when I wanted a third ear piercing and they advised against it because it would become very obvious how uneven my ears are, which I had never noticed in the first place. Weird, right?

Every decision we make every day has an effect on our bodies. I'm positive you've heard the advice that first thing in the morning you should drink lemon water, or warm water with salt, or celery juice, or some other thing meant to help your body perform at the optimum level (whatever that means for you). The choices you make from day to day have a collective effect on your body in the future.

Our bodies are essentially just squishy machines with bones that both keep us from being a blob. It's all pretty cool and pretty gross if you think about it.

Yet with all of this going on, we still find ways to belittle our bodies and worse, the bodies of other people. We look at bodies and don't think, "Look at that little miracle walking around! Incredible!" Instead we tend to be critical. A large part of that is likely us projecting our own hang ups and insecurities onto others. If we see someone whose body looks the way we'd like our own to look, we may feel shame or anger at ourselves for *not* looking that way.[6] And some people criticize just to feel better about themselves for a brief moment, to feel superior.

That's a lot of wasted effort just to judge someone so we feel better in one way or another. Instead, why not use that effort to look inward and say something positive about ourselves? The next time you have a critical thought about someone else's body, stop yourself and say one nice thing about your own. "Hey, you scientific marvel, there's no one else in the universe like you!"

No matter how "healthy" or "unhealthy" our bodies are, there are plenty of things to be thankful for. Bodies are the home for our being, our essence, our soul. No one knows exactly what a soul is, but whatever that ethereal quality is that makes us uniquely ourselves lives inside your body.[7] Your body makes it possible for you to hug your loved ones, to chase your dreams, to do all kinds of wonderful things.

---

[6] Harron Psy.D., Dana. "Why Do We Judge Other People?" *Psychology Today*, Sussex Publishers, www.psychologytoday.com/us/blog/living-with-eating-disorders/202110/why-do-we-judge-other-people.

[7] Lanza M.D., Robert. "Does the Soul Exist? Evidence Says 'Yes.'" *Psychology Today*, Sussex Publishers, www.psychologytoday.com/us/blog/biocentrism/201112/does-the-soul-exist-evidence-says-yes.

Can you thank your body 1% more often for all that it does for you, for giving you a vehicle to engage in the human experience? Listen to your body and see what it's telling you it needs. Take a deep breath and notice that your heart is always beating and you are always breathing even though you probably rarely think about it during the day. Bodies are truly miraculous.

Reflection

Boundaries

Protecting what's inside

Learning how to identify and develop boundaries is one of the best gifts you can give yourself. Coming from a big family (both immediate and extended) there's a lot of compromise involved in co-existing. And as I grew older, I realized that I reached adulthood with very few boundaries for myself. One of my personal guiding principles was to not disappoint people and not let my actions be a negative reflection on the larger group. However as an adult, I realized that this just led me down the path of people-pleasing and putting myself last.

A friend recommended the book, "Boundaries: When to Say Yes, How to Say No to Take Control of Your Life" and it was a much-needed welcome into the world of boundaries.[8] The funny part is I always thought I had great boundaries because I generally know how I feel and I have no problem calmly communicating that to people. But the book made me realize that I wasn't always communicating honestly with *myself*.

One analogy from the book that stuck with me and I bring to mind every time I encounter a difficult situation is the analogy of a fence. Fences help keep dangerous people out, filter who can come

---

[8] Cloud, H., & Townsend, J. (1992). *Boundaries: When to say yes, when to say no to take control of Yo*. Zondervan.

inside, and they help the people inside stay safe. *Houses have fences around them to keep the people inside safe.*

When we put up our own boundaries, we aren't being hard asses, we are just making a fence to keep ourselves safe. And we shouldn't feel bad about that!

It's also important to remember that when we enforce our boundaries, people are likely to test them. That's how fences work, too. Think about a dog encountering a fence for the first time. It wants to test out all of the weak spots to see where it can get through. People will do that with your boundaries, too. That's why it's important to know why you made the boundary in the first place. You'll need to remind yourself when there's backlash (and you must be prepared for backlash otherwise your fresh fence will crumble).

Boundaries are about safety and growth. You are always growing, and the best part is you get to choose how you are going to support that growth. You could construct fences like a competitive home gardener might, tenaciously keeping anything unwanted away from your plants and nurturing what is there, then letting in guests to visit as *you* want. Or you could be like untended grass, browning from the people walking over it all of the time, afraid to construct fences because of the inconvenience it might cause people, or because it might make the grass seem less welcoming.

The choice is yours.

Can you think of one place in your life where you can strengthen your boundaries by 1%? Can you let your team at work know that you won't be answering emails on the weekends so you can be more present with family and friends? Can you protect your sleep by going to bed at a set time every night? Can you tell someone that you don't like how they speak to you? Can you let things go to protect your peace?

There are almost endless boundaries we can put up, so start with one that feels relevant today. The others will present themselves as time goes on, but start small. It's one of the best gifts you'll ever give yourself.

Reflection

Breath

Your anchor is always with you

Take a moment while you're reading this and just notice the fact that you're breathing. You don't even have to think about it because your body is automatically making sure that you're breathing, that you're bringing in clean, fresh oxygen and exhaling carbon dioxide.

Tuning into our breath is one of the most powerful tools we have available to us at all times, and we can use it almost like a kind of medicine. If you've never heard of breathwork, that's okay. It's essentially using the power of the breath to achieve various sensations in the body. For example, if you're feeling ungrounded or stressed, you can try a box breath. Inhale through your nose for the count of four, hold your breath for the count of four, exhale through your nose for the count of four, and hold for four before inhaling and starting the count over again. After a few rounds of this, you'll notice you're feeling calmer. If you really need to ease some anxiety, exhale for twice as long as you inhale. Or conversely if you want to get some energy, you can do a "fire breath" where you forcefully exhale the air through your nose then let your body reflexively inhale before you forcefully exhale again. After a few rounds, you will feel more energy flowing through your body.

So, why am I including an entire chapter about breath in this book? Because it's a great way to help us regulate our nervous system and emotions without needing anything at all. You don't have to wait until later to feel better. It can happen right now. It's also something you can do without drawing attention to yourself. Let's pretend you're in a stressful meeting. Stretching or moving around may make you feel better by getting some of that anxious energy out, but it's likely not appropriate in that setting. Luckily, a simple box breath exercise can help you calm down and no one will even know that you're doing it.

Or even simpler, you can say in your mind to yourself, "I am breathing." This has become my go-to strategy. When I'm in a frustrating situation and can feel myself getting tense, I stop the thoughts spiraling around and think, "I am breathing." It helps remove me from the emotion of the situation, tune into my body for a second or two, and have a moment of gratitude that I am breathing. Even though the atmosphere around me may feel intense, this quick escape in my brain helps bring me back to the present and focus on what's actually important: I am alive. I am breathing. I am grateful that my body is breathing without me needing to do anything.

When you're focused on your breathing, you're not worrying about what happened in the past or what might happen in the future. You're just simply being and breathing.

Can you start trying to pay attention to your breath 1% more of the time? Maybe when you're stuck in traffic, in the shower, or on a walk. Notice how your natural breathing cadence feels, or how you feel if you change it up. The more you can sit with your breath, the calmer you'll be and you'll feel more connected to your body.

Reflection

Chaos

Using disorder to your benefit

When you think of chaos, chances are good it doesn't strike a happy chord within you. For many people, chaos and the disorder it brings is like a circle of hell. When your alarm doesn't go off, so you and your kids are running late, then you realize you forgot to get fuel in the car but you also can't find your keys… You get the idea. Or think of any movie where they show the state of a house after a raucous college party. That is all chaos.

But what if I told you a little bit of chaos can be something good that you use to your advantage?

When things are in disarray, we have lots of options for how to respond, all of which help us hone our decision making and flex our resilience. If we are in a situation that is unfolding in an unexpected way, we have the opportunity to get creative with how to address it.

Let's go with the houseparty example. Pretend the kitchen is a mess and every dish has been emptied from the cabinets. That gives the people who use the kitchen a perfect reason to rethink the way their room is organized or to do a spring cleaning. Maybe it even prompts them to clean out the "junk drawer" that is a staple in every kitchen.

Chaos gives us a chance to have a fresh start, to make a new beginning out of disorder.

In Greek mythology, Chaos is one of the hardest figures to understand. It is considered the first entity that existed, representing a void from which everything else came to be. It is empty and formless, the perfect blank canvas. And sure enough, according to the mythology, everything that has come to pass was born out of that infinite abyss.

Chaos doesn't need to be cosmic to present itself in your own life. As mentioned, there are plenty of everyday happenings that can create their own tiny worlds of chaos. So keep in mind that each of those moments is a chance for you to choose what you will create out of them. Will you create a more present, attentive version of yourself, or maybe you'll find optimism in what the disaster can surface. Personally, I like finding the creativity in the chaos; how can I take this problem with new parameters and come up with the most elegant solution?

Finding peace and grounding in the chaos is hard. As you'll learn throughout this book, our brains like to keep us safe, so they make us feel anxious in new and different scenarios. If the idea of chaos is throwing you off, not to worry; that's totally normal.

The important piece to keep in mind is that life is chaotic. We can make as many plans as we want, but we can't 100% predict what will happen each day. There's always room for a little bit of chaos to sneak in, and that's when it's your time to shine.

Though it may be hard in the moment, try to find peace and calm when there's madness around you. See if you can approach a chaotic moment with a thoughtful solution or a creative way to reframe what's going on. Managing even 1% more of the chaos in your life will start feeling like a superpower over time.

Reflection

Codependence

What are secretly dependent on?

Years ago, one of my sisters sent me the book "Codependent No More" because she insisted that I was codependent on working. At the time, I wasn't ready to hear that feedback and the book, which was meant to be helpful, was quickly shelved. Fast-forward years, maybe even a decade, and I was very burned out, unable to find joy in practically anything. I started searching for answers to what was going on with me and it turned out... I was codependent on work. Exactly what she'd tried to save me from years prior. And yes, I did end up reading and loving that book.

When we think of "codependence" we may think of addictions, toxic relationships, or unhealthy habits. Rarely do we realize that sometimes we can also become codependent on things that are necessary, good, or helpful to us.

How might codependency show up in your life in unexpected ways? Might you be codependent on stress? I used to joke that stress was the glue that held my mom together. She was very much a person who would be having a perfectly good time, then bring up some worry that just popped into her mind.

Might you be codependent on work? Maybe beyond a paycheck, you find identity in your work or in the success that your work offers you. For me, I loved the hit of dopamine I'd get when I saw my name on a published article, so I was always chasing after more bylines. What would it look like if you separated yourself from your "job" and started discovering what it is about being you that brings you joy.

How can you get rid of 1% of your hidden codependencies? Or how can you begin to discover 1% more of them? Codependency is sneaky, so be on the lookout.

Reflection

Commitment

Honoring your commitments honors yourself

We often hear about "commitment" through the lens of committing to others, but the more I started thinking about it, all commitments at their core are personal. We commit to all kinds of things: events, actions, people. But if you boil it down, you are at the center of every commitment that you make.

And when you don't honor your commitments, it's less about disappointing others and more about letting yourself down, even if it doesn't feel like it at the moment.

For example, you committed to meeting up with a friend, but at the last minute, you have to back out. You may feel bad for letting your friend down, and on a deeper level you're bummed because you deprived yourself of the opportunity to hang out.

Let's think about it on an even smaller level: your commitments to yourself. How many times have you said you're going to wake up early and do X, Y, Z and then never actually do it? Chances are, it's more than you can count. You're not alone, by the way.

But every time we do that, we signal to ourselves that we don't value ourselves enough to keep our personal commitments. It's common advice that if you want to have a regular workout routine, schedule it in your calendar and treat it like a doctor's appointment or a work meeting. Why is that? Because we move mountains to make sure our schedules can accommodate these types of appointments and meetings, but we often don't show our own selves the same respect.

This is one of the biggest areas in my life where I can improve. I'll get a new idea, get excited, write out a whole plan, and then BOOM life happens and I can't follow through. Or maybe the plan was never realistic in the first place. And all of the times this has happened, I'm demonstrating to myself that I'm not as important as other commitments in my life. How sad is that? Can you start considering 1% more of your commitment making process? Are you making realistic commitments that you actually plan on following through with or are you being a bit frivolous? It's great to be aspirational, but maybe you can temper the commitments that come with those aspirations. For example, if you want to start eating healthier, commit to doing it for three days, not "the rest of your life." Set yourself up to honor your commitments by starting small and being more mindful about them.

Reflection

Community

We all need each other

I am a huge introvert. Sometimes I can physically feel the energy draining from my body when I'm with a group of people. It has nothing to do with who is in the group — I love my friends and am always grateful when our schedules align. But the way I'm wired means I recharge by being alone with myself and my own thoughts. So when I used to hear the word "community" I'd cringe and think, "No! Please! Not a group of people! That's not for me."

But over time, I've come to understand that community can mean something different for us all while still serving the same purpose.[9] According to one study, a sense of community is "increasingly being recognized as an important determinant of health." And the CDC cites that it can help prevent heart disease, dementia, anxiety, and depression as well as improve overall quality of life.

A real life example of this is "blue zones." Blue zones are places in the world where people regularly live to 100 years or more. The zones have a lot in common with each other including a clear sense of community.[10] "Ikigai: The Japanese Secret to a Long and Happy

---

[9] Michalski, Camilla A, et al. "Relationship between Sense of Community Belonging and Self-Rated Health across Life Stages." *U.S. National Library of Medicine,* U.S. National Library of Medicine, 12 Oct. 2020, pmc.ncbi.nlm.nih.gov/articles/PMC7585135/.
[10] "Lessons from the Blue Zones®." *Business Engagement in Building Healthy Communities: Workshop Summary.*, U.S. National Library of Medicine, 8 May 2015, www.ncbi.nlm.nih.gov/books/NBK298903/.

Life" is one of my favorite books and details how it's possible to live a long, healthy life, including daily integration of community. In many blue zones, they end their day by congregating at the local social house (whatever that looks like for their particular culture) to swap stories from the day and just hang out for a while.[11]

So, what does community look like in our busy everyday lives and how can we cultivate community that feels more aligned with us individually?

For many people, this answer is easy. You simply gravitate towards a group that shares similar interests and that's your community. This might be related to your religion, your work, your hobbies, where your child goes to school, where you live, or any number of things. Whether you're in the HOA, the PTA, or the CIA, you can find community in all of those places. Websites like Meet-Up make it easy to find people with like minded interests, and the options have broadened thanks to tools like Zoom.

Even if you're introverted and find too much socializing to be draining, it's still important to get out there and be social. It doesn't have to be a lot, maybe just volunteering once or twice a month, or joining an online community that allows you to participate on your own time. You could take a class to learn a new skill or maybe even teach a skill somewhere local. I like to embroider, and during the pandemic I was asked to teach an online workshop for a group of

---

[11] García, Héctor, et al. *Ikigai: The Japanese Secret to a Long and Happy Life*. Penguin Books, 2017.

people at work. When we returned to the office, it turned into a monthly chat where we shared the projects we were working on, tips and tricks, and whatever else is on people's minds. This meet-up is one of the community events I genuinely look forward to. Volunteering also offers all different levels of socialization from being really extroverted, like hosting events, to more solitary, like picking up trash at the beach with an organization.

Inclusion of online spaces in the concept of community is very important to recognize as well. The 2008 documentary *Second Skin* perfectly shows how gamers get a bad rap for being anti-social when in reality they are building communities with people all over the world, it's just in a virtual context. Some people live in rural areas, don't have access to reliable transportation, have disabilities, or have any other number of reasons why physically engaging in community may be hard for them. That's why it's always a good idea to keep accessibility of communities in mind when organizing them.

So this week, how can you engage in community 1% more? Can you find an online community that only requires a level of participation you're comfortable with? Can you volunteer for an organization that does something you're interested in? Can you engage more deeply with some of the acquaintanceships you already have and broaden your personal community that way? The more you embrace community, the better chance you give yourself at having a longer happy, healthy life.

Reflection

Comparison

The thief of joy

I've practiced yoga since I was 16 years old, but there are some very simple things that I just can't do. Sitting back on my heels is one of them. I talked to my podiatrist about it and asked what I can do to gain that ability. He explained that my body just isn't put together in a way that makes that particular pose possible without exacerbating other issues (plantar fasciitis!).

Then he told me a story about Jacki Sorensen, a pioneer of aerobics dance classes. She didn't like having mirrors in her classes because people would compare themselves to others in the class. Without mirrors, they did what they individually were capable of and had no idea how they looked doing it. This helped keep them coming back because the classes made them feel awesome, and not like they weren't quite as talented as Pink Leotard in the front row. In their minds, they were equal to Pink Leotard.

Comparing ourselves and our abilities to others robs us of feeling good in our own bodies and with our own progress. Even if it sparks a temporary good feeling, that may just be us feeling superior.

Research shows that while some comparison can give your ego a boost and motivate you to do more, in general, comparison can be pretty detrimental. It's called Social Comparison Theory and it "shows that people who regularly compare themselves to others may experience feelings of dissatisfaction, guilt, or remorse."[12] Upward comparison is when we compare ourselves to those who we think are better than us. Downward comparison is when we compare ourselves to those who we think are lower than us. Either way, without lots of mental discipline, comparison can become an overall negative slippery slope.

So, why not avoid comparison in general? You are uniquely you. No one else has walked the same path as you, every minute of every day. Your body is unique. Your life is unique. Everything about you is singularly and wonderfully you.

You only have your life to live. So don't waste time comparing yourself to someone else!

The next person is not your own measuring stick. And certainly no one on social media, TV, etc. should be what you aim to measure up to. Those are curations that people show to the world. Influencers are trying to sell you a dream. No matter how inspirational or hardcore they seem, always remember they are selling you a lifestyle. Why would you compare yourself to a carefully crafted sales pitch?

I'll give you an example of comparison that I grapple with at least a few times each year. "I feel like I'm doing this journaling thing wrong." This is what I say to myself every time I once again try to "discover the wonders of journaling." Despite being a writer, I'm

---

[12] "Social Comparison Theory." *Psychology Today*, Sussex Publishers, www.psychologytoday.com/us/basics/social-comparison-theory.

not a journaler. I've tried all of the techniques, but I don't feel whatever magic it is people say they feel from journaling. So, after the latest round of attempting to be a journaler, I found myself thinking I'm doing it wrong.

But then I thought about it more... How can I be JOURNALING wrong? There's no right or wrong way to journal. Everyone has their own method, their own desired outcome, their own everything. It may be possible that journaling just isn't for me. And that's okay! It doesn't mean I've fundamentally failed as a human being because I don't like journaling.

Some people are morning people, some people are night people, some people have kids, some don't, some have nannies or other forms of help, some people have invisible illnesses... the list goes on and on as to how we're different in ways we may never know. Even two kids with the same parents don't have the same childhood. They each experience it from their own lens and their own frame of reference.

If you take only one thing away from this topic, please make it this: you will never know every detail of someone else's life. So why compare yourself to them? And if we're all trying to know ourselves a little more every day, what makes you think that they even know themselves well enough to be someone you should strive to be like?

You can be 1% better by striving to be *YOUR* best you. When you find yourself in a comparison spiral, stop and remind yourself that you are really freaking special. You are the only one of you ever, in all of history. You are incomparable.

Reflection

Confidence

Everything you need is already within you

Confidence is one of my favorite themes to work with because it's something that people can reach for in the blink of an eye. If you're doing a big presentation at work, you psych yourself up to have the confidence to get through it. If you have to do something athletic for the first time in years, you give yourself a pep talk. Even if you have to make a phone call you don't want to, you take a deep breath and go for it.

We can all conjure confidence at the drop of a hat. It's the old "fake it 'til you make it" strategy.

So, why do we struggle with it so much on a daily basis?

The first thing is to ask yourself *why* you're seeking confidence in the area in which you are. For example, I don't need to have the confidence of a tennis pro because I'm not seeking any kind of achievement. However, I can tell myself that I am capable of playing and winning a game of tennis. And that one little reassurance builds over time and eventually I'll start believing I can win without even needing the pep talk.

Confidence is also linked to "imposter syndrome" (discussed later on in the book). But I love this conversation because here's the thing: the first time anyone does something for the first time is… the same for everyone! You've never walked until you learn how to walk. When babies learn how to walk they aren't thinking, "Oh no, I don't think I can walk very well because Baby Kate walked sooner than me so she's obviously better." Babies just stay in their lane and work up towards walking until one day, they walk!

Adults are the same way, but the problem is that we have the disadvantage of comparison, and comparison makes us want to quit, or think that we're not "good."

This is where confidence comes in. Have the confidence in yourself and in your life experience to know that you have lived through and overcome every challenging moment in your life so far.

The next time a tough situation comes up, can you give yourself a little 1% boost to know you'll get through it? Approach life from a place of power, not a place of fear, because no matter the outcome, you were brave enough to get started, to take that first step, and that's empowering!

Reflection

Conflict

Finding growth in hard moments

While there are some people who enjoy conflict, I'd wager that the vast majority of us don't wake up in the morning looking for a fight. In fact, most people probably shy away from conflict, sometimes to their own detriment.

But the thing is that a little conflict every now and then is good for us.

As the name would suggest, conflict gives us the opportunity to practice conflict resolution which is probably more prevalent in your life than you realize. If you have children, you're likely to negotiate small conflicts with them all day long, whether they want to watch another show, stay up late, or don't want to eat their vegetables. You may encounter someone who treated you unkindly, or have an unmeetable deadline at work that wasn't part of your plan. Or maybe you encountered some genuinely unpleasant conflict that requires some pretty strong conflict resolution muscles.

All of these offer us opportunities to get better at dealing with conflict and realizing that conflict is an important part of the human experience. We *all* need to learn to get along with each other.

I try really hard to do a good job when I'm working, and when I fail to do something, I used to take it personally. This made receiving feedback feel almost confrontational to me. But as time went on I learned that these moments weren't meant to be conflicts at all. They were just a normal part of life at work. It slowly helped me learn the difference between conflict and conversation.

Conflicts can teach us a lot about our communication styles as well as how others communicate. Some people may have a straightforward approach while others get to the point in a roundabout way. Understanding each other's styles can help both parties approach the issue from a neutral place.

Compassion is another takeaway from conflict. Sometimes all that we can see is our own side of the issue, which is normal. But it's not great for relationships, so by talking things out, we're able to understand where someone else is coming from. Maybe there was some tension because someone was going through a personal issue. It's good to come to an understanding about that so no one carries resentment.

On the other hand, conflict helps us release attachments to the outcome of a situation, especially the outcome of being liked by people. How many times during a conflict have you sacrificed what you really believed and wanted just so that you're still liked by the time the conversation winds down? But if we release ourselves from aiming for a particular outcome and "ride the wave" of the conflict, then we are able to stay true to ourselves.

Conflicts also give us the opportunity to practice listening instead of thinking to respond. There's an old saying that we have two ears and one mouth because we should listen more than we talk. But it's very common to think about how you're going to respond to someone even before they've finished talking. In conflict resolution, it's important to listen to what the other person is saying instead of thinking that you already know what they are going to say. Otherwise you'll start forming what you're going to say, or any of the other things your mind may start doing when you're supposed to be listening. When that happens, we miss the nuances of the argument someone is making and can lose a crucial piece of what they're trying to share with you.

Try getting 1% more comfortable with conflict and think about how it helps us become better versions of ourselves. What are you learning each time that you're in conflict? Learning to use conflict as a tool can be super beneficial in the long run.

Reflection

Connection

Connecting is foundational

Community is part of connecting, and there's a previous chapter on that, but connection is so much more. Obviously, we are socially connected now more than ever before thanks to the everpresent tiny computers in our hands and on our wrists. But I challenge you to think about the quality of those connections and how you connect to other aspects of your life.

Thinking about your food is a great way to do this. Let's say you're eating a simple garden salad. Think about that lettuce and everything that went into getting it onto your table. From the farmers to the pickers to the packagers, the people who make the packaging, the people involved in shipping, then there's the store owners and employees where you bought the lettuce from… and that's just the lettuce! Thinking about all of the connections for the ingredients in any dressing will take you longer than it would to finish the meal.

Whether you live in a city or small town, you're connected with everyone around you. Try setting off fireworks for 15 minutes in the middle of the night on a weeknight if you want to test the theory and see how many people come outside to let you know how your noise is affecting them. You're nearly guaranteed to hear from a few folks you've never talked to before.

If you know anyone who plays video games then you know they may play with the same people for decades and never actually meet the people in person, but they're still connected thanks to the group of creators who made that game a reality and those who engineered the consoles used to play the games.

Ironically, because the internet has let us believe we live in our little bubbles, we've lost touch with just how connected we are with each other and with the world around us.

Go to a local park and look around, keeping in mind all of the decades, maybe even centuries, of work that have gone into creating that public space and allocating the resources to maintain it, just so we can all find a nice little piece of nature when we need it.

If you're feeling alone, lackadaisical, disconnected, or any host of other emotions, pick just one item around you. It could be something as simple as your shirt or your water cup. Now think about all of the time and effort that went into design, creation, distribution, etc. Simply by existing in your environment, that item has connected you with hundreds of people!

Can you be 1% more mindful of your connections in this world today, and can you show them gratitude? Can you stop for just a moment to honor all of the connections that needed to take place in order for you to be existing in this moment right now, just as you are. And can you think about how you're connecting with others and how you might do that in a more meaningful way? Maybe you can text that friend you keep thinking about "just to say hi," or maybe you can send a simple card to someone, or even just make a $10 donation to a cause that is important to you. When we honor our connections, the world comes alive.

Reflection

Consistency

The unlikely key to being consistent

No matter what success book or article you read, there's one recurring piece of advice: Be consistent.

This is something I have struggled with my entire life. I can be consistent for a specific amount of time, but long term consistency? That has not been my strength. And once I lose focus or momentum, it can be hard to find my way back. I also feel embarrassed about the visibility that can come with not being consistent. That's why when people start a diet or some other program, they are encouraged to tell people in their lives to help them stay accountable. Or in other words, using peer pressure to stay consistent.

But believe it or not, "falling off the wagon" of consistency is okay. It's actually a good indicator of something being out of whack when consistency comes into question.

According to consistency theory, consistency is described as the "compatibility of many simultaneously transpiring mental processes," and is a systemic demand, on a neural level, for harmonious neural flow.[13] When the relationship between

---

[13] Vincent, Alessia M, et al. "Motive Satisfaction in Chronic Pain Patients: Does It Improve in Multidisciplinary Inpatient Treatment and, If so, Does It Matter?" *Journal of Clinical Psychology in Medical Settings*, U.S. National Library of Medicine, June 2021, pmc.ncbi.nlm.nih.gov/articles/PMC8192351/.

intrapsychic processes and states are harmonious, there is a state of consistency.

In other words, no matter how badly you want to be consistent with something, you'll always struggle if:
- the task itself is out of harmony with your daily life
- something is out of harmony with what you actually want
- it's just not realistic (and that's okay if it isn't)

I know I'm not alone in feeling like once consistency has gone by the wayside, so has all of the progress that I made in that time.

That's not true at all!

Being consistent is about more than the desired outcome of the thing we're pursuing. It's about what happens to our brains during that time of pursuit.

Believe it or not, we have a tremendous amount of power over our brains. That may feel like a flat out lie to anyone who struggles with anxiety, but it's true. We have the power to slowly, incrementally make changes to our neural pathways. If you've heard of neuroplasticity, that's what I'm talking about.[14]

It's important to know that our brains *do not* like change. They don't like anything for which they don't already have a frame of reference. It's part of our healthy anxiety response. So any time you want to start something new, whether it's a new routine, a new fitness program, or a new hobby, your brain is going to resist. It is

---

[14] Mannino, Emma. "How to Rewire Your Brain." *Center for Healthy Aging*, 30 Aug. 2023, www.research.colostate.edu/healthyagingcenter/2022/05/31/how-to-rewire-your-brain/.

going to come up with reasons why you should stop because it's uncomfortable.[15]

So when you want to start waking up earlier, writing every day, going on a daily walk, cooking dinner every night, etc. just know that your brain is going to tell you "this is too hard." It's doing that because the consistent activity is new and uncomfortable.

But life happens and even though you've been consistent for a few days, a few weeks, or longer, something might occur and your shiny new routine goes by the wayside. And the worst enabler in letting this happen was your brain.

Does that mean you made no progress during the time when you were consistent? Not at all. And there are two big reasons why.

First, back to the brain. You have laid the foundation (neural pathways) for these habits and routines to become ingrained. They are no longer foreign to your brain. And while there may have been some discomfort at first, this new habit/activity isn't brand new anymore. "It's like riding a bike." Riding a bike the second time is always easier than the first because you know you can do it.

Second, life isn't a video game. You don't lose all of your progress and go back to the beginning. If you did something as small as swapped chips for veggies as an afternoon snack, your body won't instantly deplete of all the extra nutrients you gave it on the previous days. If you were reading every night before bed, your

---

[15] Spector, Nicole. "How to Train Your Brain to Accept Change, According to Neuroscience." *NBCNews.Com*, NBCUniversal News Group, 12 Nov. 2018, www.nbcnews.com/better/health/how-train-your-brain-accept-change-according-neuroscience-ncna934011.

brain still reaped the rewards of that activity (and your sleep probably improved too).

What all of this means is that consistency makes a difference, even if our ability to achieve consistency is inconsistent. And remember, it looks different for all of us on any given day.

What can you be 1% more consistent with? It can be small – making your bed, stretching, or drinking more water. And how can you be gentle with yourself in your overall lifelong pursuit of consistency?

Reflection

Creativity

Everybody's so creative

Through conversations, I've found that lots of folks are down on themselves when it comes to the creativity department. They have put themselves in a box where they either are or aren't a creative person. And that is so sad because we are all creative!

There is a hilarious TikTok creator Tanara Mallory who coined the catchphrase "everybody's so creative" on her videos where she watches people cook some truly wild meals. But I love that there is truth within the joke.

Everybody IS so creative! And it's important to flex that muscle, no matter if you think you're creative or not.

Here are some benefits to expressing your creative side:[16,17]

- It helps process difficult emotions
- It helps recover from traumatic events
- It helps you access your "flow state"
- It helps treat dementia
- It helps overall mental wellbeing

---

[16] Stahl, Ashley. "Here's How Creativity Actually Improves Your Health." *Forbes*, Forbes Magazine, 20 Feb. 2024, www.forbes.com/sites/ashleystahl/2018/07/25/heres-how-creativity-actually-improves-your-health/?sh=328ae17213a6.

[17] Field, Barbara. "How Creativity Positively Impacts Your Health." *Verywell Mind*, Verywell Mind, 23 Mar. 2021, www.verywellmind.com/how-creativity-positively-impacts-your-health-5113162.

- It helps make you smarter

Sounds great, right? And now you may be thinking, "Natalie, we're adults. I'm not going to learn to be an artist at my age." Well good news: You don't have to learn anything new or spend any money to start being creative today. I'll never forget when we were kids and our parents told one of my sisters she needed a creative outlet. She looked straight at them and said, "My outfit is my creative outlet!" tossed her hair, and walked off like she was on a runway.

But even if fashion isn't your outlet, there are some very accessible ways to be creative right now:

- Take pictures on your phone from a different angle than you normally use (I like to switch to my front camera and take pictures of the sky to get a different perspective)
- Edit a picture that's already on your phone
- Doodle (you can throw it away and no one has to see it if you're embarrassed)
- Make (or even just plate) a "fancy" meal
- Dance!

On the flip side, people who are highly creative can experience burnout. I recently heard a professional artist talk about how we treat artists like this never-ending fount of creative inspiration. But that's not the case. Artists need a break from their normal art forms in order to recharge and recover. If that's you, here are some ways to still express yourself while recovering:

- Try a new form of art

- Take a class to learn a totally new skill
- Dance!
- Or maybe even do nothing! When you feel drained, sometimes you just need time for your reserves to refill.

Finding small ways to be creative can alter your day and offer long term benefits. **Find one opportunity each day to be creative. No one has to know you did it. This is for you! You've got this!**

Reflection

Curiosity

Curiosity cured the cat

You may have heard the saying that "curiosity killed the cat" but have you ever heard that "curiosity cured the cat?" Back in 1928, Alexander Fleming was trying to find a way to treat staphylococci bacteria. One day, the Scottish biologist noticed that there was mold growing in the petri dish and it was inhibiting the spread of the bacteria. He studied the mold and the drug penicillin was born. Instead of tossing out his experiment, he got curious and developed one of the most widely used healing drugs in history.

Throughout history, there are countless examples of how curiosity led to incredible discoveries. But in our busy world, it can be hard to find the time to be curious, which is a real shame because our brain rewards us when we stop and explore the concepts we're interested in. When we are internally motivated to be curious our brain sends out little hits of dopamine.[18] Internally motivated means we want to explore a topic because we're actually intrigued as opposed to external motivation, like trying to find the answer to a test question. So, the more we look into things that pique our interest, the happier we become. But if we don't explore the things we're curious about, we miss out on that reward from our brain, and we also miss out on other long lasting benefits like the ability to

---

[18] Encyclopædia Britannica, inc. (n.d.). *The Science of Curiosity*. Encyclopædia Britannica. https://curiosity.britannica.com/science-of-curiosity.html

enhance how we learn. Being curious helps us develop the skills to learn new concepts more efficiently than if we weren't trying to find the answers to our most burning questions.

If you don't even know where to get started with curiosity, you can start by just noticing what's around you or question why something happened, like Fleming did with the mold. You can question why an event occurs, which is how many of our laws of physics were discovered. You can also think about how one concept can be applied to another field, like how Guttenberg used the concept of a wine press to make the printing press.

Every single one of us has a unique mind and unique thoughts that we can bring to the table. Just imagine how many questions you can come up with if you allowed yourself the time to get curious.

Anyone who has been around little kids in their "why" stage knows how exhausting it can get to answer the barrage of "why" questions, but imagine if you still let yourself have that kind of childlike wonder. Start allowing yourself to get curious about the world around you, because you never know what could become of it. Think about the last time you went down a rabbit hole and how excited you were to share the knowledge with someone else.

Can you give yourself permission to follow your next "why" thought and investigate it? If you aren't naturally curious, can you be 1% more conscious of looking for moments in your daily life that make you stop and wonder, then follow through on that wonder to try and get some answers? When we flex our curiosity muscle, we not only make ourselves feel better but we also flex our mental learning muscle. It's a win-win for you, and depending on where your curiosity leads you, maybe a win for the world, too.

Reflection

Daydreaming

Solving unsolvable problems

When you were young, you were probably told once or twice to stop daydreaming and pay attention. So it's no wonder that as adults who have a much longer "to do" list than kids and teens, we don't allow ourselves to daydream. We've got to "get back to work."

And that's not a good thing. It turns out daydreaming is really beneficial in practical — and sometimes actionable — ways.

It may *feel* like you're staring at nothing and your brain is turned off, but in fact it's fired up in ways that are difficult to achieve outside of daydreaming. Your executive network of your brain is still working even though you've essentially tapped into your default mode network.[19]

So what does this mean? While you're drifting off into daydreamland, your brain is still working on solving problems but it is able to do so in a more creative way since the pressure to solve a problem *this very second* is gone.

Rick Rubin, legendary music producer, talks about this in his book "The Creative Act: A Way of Being."[20] When he leaves the

---

[19] "The Benefits of Daydreaming - Elizabeth Cox." *TED*, TED-Ed, ed.ted.com/lessons/the-benefits-of-daydreaming-elizabeth-cox.
[20] Rubin, Rick, and Neil Strauss. *The Creative Act: A Way of Being*. Penguin Press, 2023.

studio, he also leaves behind any problems he's trying to solve with regard to a particular song or project. Then he may work on a completely different project or just go about his day. Either way, he's freeing his brain from the pressure to solve the problem, and though it may seem counterintuitive, the answer will usually come to him.

Now, in fairness to science, there is a point of mind-wandering that is detrimental.[21] This is typically when we start dwelling on the past or worrying about the future. And we all know those two things aren't helpful. But if you're doing an activity you enjoy or that helps you stay present — going for a walk, washing dishes, etc. — you are more easily able to tap into the sweet spot of daydreaming. This is why people say they come up with their best ideas in the shower.

Or as John Kounios — professor of psychology and co-author of "The Eureka Factor: Aha Moments, Creative Insight, and the Brain" — explains, we can analytically solve a problem or we can solve it through insight. But insight comes when we disconnect from the conscious mind.[22]

Ok, so you're sold on the value of constructive daydreaming, but how do you induce it?

---

[21] *Why Do We Get Our Best Ideas in the Shower? - The Washington Post*, www.washingtonpost.com/wellness/2023/01/12/shower-thoughts-creativity-brain/

[22] "Why Do We Get Our Best Ideas in the Shower?" *Headspace*, www.headspace.com/articles/shower-epiphanies.

You can start with a process similar to mindfulness meditation. Close your eyes, take a couple of deep breaths, then think about something you like. It could be anything. A funny memory, a place you want to visit, just think of the thing and let your mind drift from there.

Another method is to go outside and simply observe what's going on around you. If you start thinking about something, let your thoughts drift. Since you are in a new environment with different stimuli than you were when you were actively problem solving, you'll have a better chance at coming up with a creative solution or a fun thought.

When I'm able to, I like to employ an old school method of daydreaming: find a nice lawn to lay down on and make shapes out of the clouds. My brain is engaged in a way that lets it float around.

Try making 1% more effort to free your mind! Intentionally set aside some time to daydream, especially if you have a problem you're trying to solve or if everything feels totally overwhelming. Tap into your thoughts and see what kind of journey they reveal.

Reflection

Decisions

What guides your decisions?

We're faced with thousands of choices every day. But after you've weighed the choices, you have to make a decision. Which means our days are really just a collection of decisions. Let's assume you sleep for eight hours. That means you have 57,600 seconds in the day, and you are making decisions for the majority of those seconds, whether you realize it or not.

One study sought to figure out how just how many daily decisions we make and how many we're aware of making:[23]

"Researchers at Cornell University estimate we make 226.7 decisions each day on food alone. And as your level of responsibility increases, so does the multitude of choices you have to make. It's estimated that the average adult makes about 35,000 remotely conscious decisions each day. Each decision, of course, carries certain consequences with it that are both good and bad."

So what is guiding your decisions? What criteria are you basing these decisions on? It has to be something.

What is your North Star? What is driving your decisions? If you can't think of it, then spend some time figuring out what to align your decisions toward. Point yourself in the right direction for you.

---

[23] Graff, Frank. "How Many Decisions Do We Make in One Day?" *PBS North Carolina*, PBS North Carolina, 10 Aug. 2022, www.pbsnc.org/blogs/science/how-many-decisions-do-we-make-in-one-day/.

Take stock of how often your decisions align with that North Star. If it's more often than not, great! You're on the right track. If not, then you know you have 35,000 self-directed opportunities today to get back on track. Then 35,000 more tomorrow. Over time, those may become habits and trickle to the 20,000+ choices you subconsciously make every day, too!

If you need help figuring out what your North Star is, think both big and small. Do you want to be a more engaged parent? Do you want to be a more thoughtful friend? Do you want to be kinder to yourself? Do you want to embark on a learning journey that you feel will be enriching? Do you just want to be a bit more tidy? Think about Future You and what that person looks and feels like. What lifestyle does Future You live? What decisions were made today to get Future You to that place?

And with all of this, be gentle with yourself. Life goals and desires change as time goes on. Your goal right now may not be your goal in a few months or a few years. That's why it's good to check in with yourself to see if your actions are lining up with your desired outcome.

Take time to evaluate 1% more of your decisions. Spend a day observing how you're deciding between several choices and think about if they're aligning with what's really important to you.

Reflection

Disappointment

Moving on from disappointing yourself and others

Well, I hate to say this but once again I did not win the lotto. And I was very disappointed. I did all of the things social media told me to do (speaking it into existence, etc.) and yet, I am not a Powerball millionaire.

I'm trying to add levity to something that's a very real, very emotional experience people have: disappointment. But it's on purpose. Did you know that disappointment is something our brain makes us feel and the best way to combat it is to do things that feel good? Let me back up...

While disappointment hasn't been studied as much as regret, they've been able to quantify the spectrum of disappointment.[24,25] When you are disappointed, two neurotransmitters fire at the same time that land you somewhere along the spectrum of "oh well" to "total bummer."

Neurotransmitters are chemicals that relay signals from one neuron to the next. The brain and nervous system use dozens of

---

[24] Tzieropoulos, Hélène, et al. "The Impact of Disappointment in Decision Making: Inter-Individual Differences and Electrical Neuroimaging." *Frontiers in Human Neuroscience*, U.S. National Library of Medicine, 6 Jan. 2011, pmc.ncbi.nlm.nih.gov/articles/PMC3020567/.

[25] Wanjek, Christopher. "Feeling Bummed? How Disappointment Works in the Brain." *LiveScience*, Purch, 25 Sept. 2014, www.livescience.com/48022-disappointment-brain.html.

neurotransmitters to enable thought and movement. Some neurotransmitters, such as dopamine and serotonin, are well-known to be associated with mood regulation. Neurons usually produce only one kind of neurotransmitter, rarely two.

In the new study, a team of scientists led by Dr. Roberto Malinow, a professor of neurobiology at the University of California, San Diego School of Medicine, found that two well-known neurotransmitters — glutamate and GABA, which is short for gamma-aminobutyric acid — are released simultaneously by neurons in a small region of the brain called the lateral habenula to signal the emotion of disappointment.[26]

One of the strangest parts of this is that the behavior people will exhibit as a result of disappointment isn't predictable. That's because not winning the lotto for one person might be an "oh well" while for another it might be "total bummer." And the way a person reacts will be different from one to the next because we are all unique people.

The gist is this: disappointment is triggered both by neurochemicals and behavioral aspects. At a base level, when disappointment strikes, you don't get the dopamine hit you anticipated. Then, you're dosed with brain chemicals that inform your brain you should be disappointed, so you are. Double brain whammy. And then societal disappointment is layered onto that

---

[26] Wanjek, Christopher. "Feeling Bummed? How Disappointment Works in the Brain." *LiveScience*, Purch, 25 Sept. 2014, www.livescience.com/48022-disappointment-brain.html.

when people may act differently towards you because you have disappointed them.

Imagine you're on an NBA team, playing in the championship. You shoot the last second shot to win annddd… you miss. Your brain is quick to fire off those chemicals to let you know you are disappointed both in yourself and in the situation. Then you have the conscious knowing you let down your teammates, the organization, the city you play for, and fans. That's a lot of disappointment to deal with, and most of it isn't even originating from your own self!

So, how do we get over disappointment? The good news is that scientists are actively studying the topic and have found that serotonin helps rebalance the way the brain processes negative events that happen to us.

And since people have been experiencing disappointment since forever, there are lots of tried-and-true ways to get over it. Here are some:

- Acknowledge the disappointment. Layering shame onto something that is already weighing on you will exacerbate the problem. If you're disappointed that you got laid off, don't hide it from people. You don't need to shout it from the rooftops either, but acknowledge it happened and move forward.
- Look at the big picture. While disappointment is very real and can have lasting effects, remind yourself that there are other things to look forward to, to be happy about. There is

no one job, one house, one person, one anything that can fulfill you and make you happy. Your life is made up of a kaleidoscope of experiences. Don't let this one thing diminish the others.

- Give yourself grace. Sometimes, despite our best efforts, events don't happen the way we planned. Very often people think they need to follow a script for life. Get married, own a house, be an executive, have kids, etc. according to a timeline that is 100% made up. Give yourself grace and space to forge your own path and do things on your own time.
- Be flexible. We've all likely heard the saying, "When one door closes, another one opens." That's true. You never know what's waiting for you if you're open to the possibilities that lay ahead.
- Manage expectations. I find that the vast majority of my disappointment stems from expectations. Here's the thing: we have very little control over life, so it doesn't make sense to expect outcomes that we have little to no impact on. Hope for the best and go with the flow, managing your expectations along the way.

Disappointment may not be one of those "what doesn't kill you makes you stronger" moments, but it can make you more compassionate towards yourself and others. It can help you practice acceptance and help you find what really brings you peace and happiness.

How can you be 1% better at facing disappointment? Can you temper potential disappointment by managing expectations? Can you show yourself kindness when it feels like others are against you? Can you remind yourself that you're human and we all make mistakes? If none of these work, then remember that disappointment is just your machine of a brain releasing chemicals, and you don't have a ton of control over this feeling. You are free to move forward whenever you're ready.

Reflection

Discipline

Find freedom through discipline

There are probably 1,000 books out there about discipline; the importance of it, the effects of it, and how to incorporate it into your own life. So, I'm not going to sit here and try to condense tons of knowledge into a bite-sized chapter, but the good news is that I don't have to in order for you to understand the benefits of discipline. And the other good news is that discipline doesn't need to be hard. In fact, if it feels hard, maybe that's a sign that you need to tweak the routine or whatever it is that you're trying to be disciplined about.

I'll start with the basic benefit of discipline which is that it actually gives you more free time. If you prepare meals at the beginning of the week, you don't need to spend time every morning packing your lunch for work because it's already done. So you get that time back. If you know that you go to the gym at a certain time, you don't waste energy bargaining with yourself about whether or not you should go, will it be too crowded, etc.

Discipline is also a great way to see results for whatever it is that you are working on, whether it's being healthier, finishing a project, or just trying to incorporate things you like into your lifestyle.

I like to make discipline as simple as possible by framing it as *not* doing something. For example, if you're trying to have the discipline to eat less takeout food, then you're just simply *not* going to buy food when you have food at home. Or if you want to work out more, then you're *not* going to skip the workout you've made time for in your schedule. If you want to go to bed earlier, you are *not* going to make the effort to stay up late. When you have a late night craving, you're going to stay planted on that couch and *not* get up to get a snack. If you're aimlessly shopping online, you're going to *not* go to your cart and go through the hassle of checking out.

When we frame discipline this way, it takes away the weight of an action we must accomplish and looks at what happens if we *don't* do that thing. It's letting yourself off the hook from having to take an action to do something, and in doing that, you are staying disciplined.

The more structure and support you can give yourself, the less things you actually *have to* do in order to stay disciplined, and in doing that, you have freedom!

Can you free up 1% of your time by choosing to be disciplined? Can you take one decision or one action off your plate just by setting yourself up for success? Where are there places in your life that you'd like to be more disciplined but aren't? Start there, and keep building.

Reflection

Drive

Drive your life at your own pace

A lot of the actions we take during the day are subconscious or biological, and we have little control over them. For example, your body makes you breathe without you thinking about it. Your brain will notice you're hungry and trigger a set of reactions to let you know that you need to eat. But what about non-essential biological factors?

To be clear, I'm not talking about motivation (which is discussed in a later chapter). I'm talking about drive. What drives you to take action? And conversely, why do you sometimes lose that drive?

In the 1940s, psychologist Clark Hull put forth the Drive-Reduction Theory (also sometimes called the Drive Theory)[27]. This is the idea that drive is a tension, arousal, or discomfort in your brain that compels your body to do something in order to reduce that feeling and return back to balance, or homeostasis. As Hull's theory became popular, people realized it still left some behavioral explanations unanswered, like why people may feel driven to take risks, which is not a basic biological function and is actually antithetical to survival.

---

[27] McFarlane, J. M. (2024, August 22). *Drive reduction theory*. Introduction to Psychology. https://opentextbc.ca/psychologymtdi/chapter/drive-reduction-theory/

Over time, the science of drive has been tied to the science of motivation, but it's still a little too simplistic to say that they're the same thing.

Many people want to make more money, get fit, have a rewarding social life, etc. which are the motivating factors, or motivation, they need. But drive is what will help them take the next step.

So, what can drive look like in your own life and how can you regulate it?

I think it's important to take a step back and think about life. No two days are the same, both in how the day plays out and in how you feel on any particular day. To illustrate, think about the actual act of your daily commute. You never see the exact same cars at the exact same times, and you may not feel the exact same way, day after day.

That's a lot like how drive in our life works. You may have all of the motivation in the world to workout in the morning, to start reading before bed, to save money, to do any number of things, but what will actually drive you to do it? How will you summon that energy, that spark you need to actually do the thing?

This made me think about a video I saw on social media where a husband filmed his wife's mental mapping of the day laid out. It went something like this: she needed to unload the dishwasher, which reminded her she needed to feed the dog, which meant she needed to go to the store to get food, and the crushed cheerios in the car needed vacuuming, which reminded her that there were no more clean towels and she needed to do laundry... you get the idea. In the end, this woman found the drive to get things done because she was doing them in service to her family. That's where she found the energy.

What is your drive for doing things? And how can you work with the natural rhythms of your life to get stuff done? I'm often asked how I do so much in a day and it humbles me because I don't feel like I do much, and often feel like I could be doing a helluva lot more. But if I had to give an honest answer, it's that I try to follow my drive instead of making my drive follow me. If I feel like writing, I write for as long as I want and check off as many things on my writing "to do" list as possible while the drive lasts. If I don't feel like running, I do strength training or yoga. Yes, of course I have deadlines and sometimes I *have to* make myself do things on time. But in general, I like to harness my drive and make it work for me as best I can, because I am positive it will wane and I'll have little-to-no warning when that happens.

It's also important to remind yourself that you're human and as such, the only things we need to do are exist and treat others (and ourselves!) as we'd like to be treated. That's it. Which is actually harder said than done to put into practice. For example, yesterday I wanted to clean out my closet and give stuff away. My motivation was weak, simply that I wanted to, and so my drive ran out about halfway through. I could have looked at myself and said, "Natalie, you're being so lazy. Just finish the closet. It'll only take another couple of hours." But would I say that someone else? Heck no! So,

I called it a day, content in the knowledge that the drive to finish the closet will arise another time, and I'll seize the moment.

We all have activities that we are naturally driven to do and others that are borderline burdensome to complete.

One way to start cultivating drive for the things you are motivated to do but can't seem to get going is to start small.

Explore how you can find 1% more drive to act on the things you're already motivated to do. Can you find small goals to set while you learn to cultivate drive? Can you capitalize on your moments of drive vs. simply checking off one task and moving on? Can you coach yourself like you'd coach a friend? Whatever it is, remember, drive is a slippery concept and no two moments will hold the same amount of drive. You're not a robot.

Reflection

Emotions

Let it out

We live in a world where it's often looked down upon to have emotions, let alone show them. God forbid one of us get emotional about something when we're in public! If women show too much emotion, we're overly sensitive or "hysterical." If men show too much emotion, they are soft or weak.

BUT NONE OF THAT IS TRUE.

We spend so much time and energy trying to push down our emotions, thinking that if we can get rid of this weakness, we'll have an edge in the world. We'll be tougher, better at navigating our way through life. But that's all a lie.

Yes, it is true that getting too *attached* to our emotions can be detrimental, but in general, both having and showing emotions is incredibly helpful not only for us but for those around us.

Let's take crying as an example. Have you ever noticed that some people start crying just from seeing someone else cry? That's because we as human beings are drawn to connect with and care for each other. It's in our wiring, so when we see someone crying, we may join in because we want to comfort them and make sure they know they aren't alone. Sometimes we cry in the subconscious hope that we will be seen.

But crying also serves some very simple biological purposes. If we're stressed, scared, anxious, etc. our bodies may start crying as a way to help regulate the parasympathetic nervous system to help us self-regulate. These tears can release oxytocin and endorphins that make us feel better. Tears have also been shown to carry stress hormones in them. So, simply by letting our body cry, we're giving into the biological need to eliminate toxins, just like if you were sweating.

I wanted to spend some time talking about the act of crying because I know so many people (me included!) can feel shame around crying when in reality, it's just an indicator our body is working like it's supposed to.

Emotions that make us cry aren't the only emotions though. If you haven't looked up an emotional wheel, take a few seconds to do so. It helps us single out and name exactly what emotion we're feeling. For example, I may feel "bad" but the wheel helps me draw out that I'm feeling stressed and ultimately overwhelmed.

When we can name our emotions, we can find more constructive ways to deal with them. It's like if someone asked you what do you want to eat and you said "food." Well, what kind of food? "Lunch." What kind of lunch food? "Something savory." You get the idea… The more you can drill down, the more you can pinpoint exactly what the need is in your life right now. Your emotions are like that. The closer you can get to what's affecting you at any moment.

If you feel like your emotions are out of control and that's why you are ashamed of them, then try using the wheel to help understand exactly what you're feeling. Remember, when our body is trying to make us show an emotion, it's not just because of some misguided "weakness;" it may be because we're craving connection, assistance, or maybe our bodies are just doing what they're supposed to do.

Can you try to name 1% more of your emotions? And can you accept that emotions are a normal part of life and nothing to be ashamed of? The more we become aware of our emotions and what triggers them the more we're able to understand ourselves and our internal lives.

Reflection

Expectations

Expect nothing of anyone

I feel like if there was one lesson I was supposed to learn in life, it's around my relationship with expectations. Our days are full of expectations, and when they aren't met, that can sometimes be a disappointing or painful moment for us.

There is a difference between hope and expectations. Hope is wanting something to happen, but sometimes we let our hope boil over into the world of expectations, and that's where trouble can come into the picture.

When I plant a garden, I hope that it grows and produces for the coming season. When it's time to harvest, if only half of my plants sprouted into something, that's okay. I hoped for the best and still got something wonderful out of it. But if I'd expected all of the plants to grow and provide all season long, I'd be disappointed when that doesn't happen. And that robs some of the joy from what did grow.

What happens in our lives is mostly out of our hands. When we layer expectations over uncertainty, we are setting ourselves up for disappointment.

Interestingly, when I searched "science behind expectations," I received results I didn't expect but that made a lot of sense. The science behind expectations is that they produce the placebo effect and can create self-fulfilling prophecies. If you've listened to any of the seemingly thousands of manifestation podcasts, they all boil down to one thing: expect good things to happen, and they will.

Well, I'm not here to say that's wrong because who knows, anything is possible. But I am here to say that when we place expectations on other people or situations (a.k.a. things that are out of our control), we are setting ourselves up for failure.

Think of all the times you've been let down by a friend, or think of times when family members say that someone didn't live up to their expectations. Social media is full of self-deprecating memes and videos of parents being disappointed with their kids for not growing up to be doctors or lawyers. Some parents pray every day and night for the kid to conform to the parent's expectations. Or in relationships where people hope the other person will change one day.

That's NOT realistic. People are who they are and that's what makes us all different.

Years ago, my friend and I went to New York City several days before Christmas and during a blizzard. We were going to get every SoCal kid's dream of seeing NYC during the holidays and in the snow! In reality, we were so cold and underdressed that we were contemplating getting right back on the plane and leaving.

Then, we finally saw the one thing everyone wants to see at that time of year: the tree at Rockefeller Center! ... But it didn't look anything like we thought it would. In fact, the entire scene was different than we'd built it up in our minds. It turned out, that's partially because it wasn't Rockefeller Center. We later learned it was Bryant Park, a place we'd never heard of. So, now we only have a picture of us in the snow in front of the Bryant Park Christmas tree and never even made it to Rockefeller Center.

My point isn't that I'm a bad traveler (though pre-Google Maps that was especially true). It's that we had unrealistic expectations for the trip — both the weather and the planning. And while we made the best of it, no amount of hoping that Bryant Park would become Rockefeller Center was going to make it true. We dropped our expectations and decided to live in the moment and survive the snow. After that, it was easily one of my favorite trips ever.

How can you release 1% more of your expectations and go with the flow? Can you impose less expectations on your friends, coworkers, family? Can you stop expecting more of your environment and find gratitude for it exactly as it is?

Reflection

Failure

Failure unlocks your potential

I'm pretty passionate about failure. Which sounds like a ridiculous thing to say, but it's true. I firmly believe that failing is a huge key to helping us unlock our potential as individuals. We live in a world that lionizes winners and where failing at anything opens you up to degradation and ridicule.

But what if we were kinder to ourselves (and to others) and allowed us to see the beauty in failure? Failure helps us get to know ourselves better, it helps us develop empathy for other people, it helps us learn and grow, and it helps us detach from outcomes.

We all know the stories of Thomas Edison failing until he created a rudimentary lightbulb. But an often untold story of failure is Winston Churchill. As a young head of the Royal Navy, he fully believed the invasion of Gallipoli in 1915 would turn the tide in the war.[28] He lobbied for the money and support to do it. In the end, nine months later, the Allies lost the battle and 250,000 people were dead. It is a tragic failure of historic proportions. As a result, Churchill resigned, joined the infantry, and worked his way up the ranks from the bottom until he was Prime Minister. He said, "All my past life had been a preparation for this hour and for this trial."

---

[28] "Winston Churchill's World War Disaster." *History.Com*, A&E Television Networks, www.history.com/news/winston-churchills-world-war-disaster.

Every failure is like every triumph: it's a brick in the building of what makes us who we are. You get to choose if that'll be a wobbly brick or a strong, foundational one.

And did you know that practicing failure can enhance your brain health and ability to learn? In his podcast *The Huberman Lab*, Dr. Andrew Huberman explains that if you spend 7-30 minutes specifically devoted to making errors and working through them, you trigger neuroplasticity in the brain, which in turn will help you learn more than if you'd quit at the first sign of failure.

So the next time you are practicing something — drawing, learning a new language, math — push through the wall of "failure" and frustration. You'll learn more even if it doesn't feel like you are in the moment.

Don't confuse this concept with the Silicon Valley "fail fast" mentality though. Failure just happens in the natural course of life, and as we all know, the natural course of life can move very slowly.

Rest assured that you are going to "fail" at something, but you get to decide how that affects you. Will you let it build you up or will you let it tear you down?

If you are scared of failure, you're not alone. I'd wager that more people are scared of failing than those that aren't. I personally only broke through my fear of failure by failing *a lot*, both professionally and personally. But it's okay! Each experience is a lesson to learn from, even if the lesson is to not take something too seriously.

So, how can you practice getting 1% more comfortable with failure?

One easy way is to set yourself up for failure. My friend once asked me why I set such intense goals for myself. I said because if I fail on the way to achieving something big, I'll have done more than if I set a reasonable goal for myself. So maybe try setting a crazy goal for yourself and see what happens.

Another way to practice failure is to use the learning scenario where you work through the wall of frustration for a while, then step away and let it go.

You could enter a contest you've been curious about for a while. Who cares if you don't win? In the scope of life, it doesn't matter. Try to solve an algebra problem just to see if you still can, and if not maybe you can re-learn the skill. Try making a new recipe. There are so many ways to try something new that have zero actual impact on your life if you fail, and then you get to take the lessons with you.

I hope this puts a lighter spin on failure for you so it isn't this heavy weight you have to carry around. Have fun with it!

Reflection

Fear

Look right at your fears

You may have seen the meme that says something to the effect of, "My nervous system doesn't know the difference between a lion chasing me and someone putting an unexpected meeting on my calendar." The list goes on of people listing the fears they have that elicit the same bodily response as an event that requires real survival.

The world can be a scary place, especially if you consume a lot of news every day. But there are other fears we've developed over time that are a daily occurrence. Did you hear about the hiker who was lost in the woods and he died because when the rescuers called him, the caller ID showed "Unknown" and he was too scared to answer? Obviously that's another joke about the silly little things that scare us, but even if they're humorous, they're no less real to the people who experience these fears.

So how do we start overcoming our fears?

Think about scary movies with a monster. They rarely ever show you the whole monster because if the audience saw whatever it was vs. only seeing flashes, it would likely take away some of the fear. The *idea* of the monster is often far scarier than what it looks like.

When we face our fears head-on, when we stop and really look at them in their fullness, they become a lot less scarier than we anticipated. Think about pain for a minute. How many times have you been injured and felt horrified thinking about the pain of cleaning a wound, recovering from surgery, etc. Sure, none of those things are pleasant, but none of them are worse than the preemptive mental pain we inflict on ourselves as we sit in fear of how bad something might hurt.

What if we started approaching fear with a "beginner's mind" and didn't work ourselves up in anticipation of how bad something might be? If you've got a review at work coming up, don't make assumptions about it. Just go in there without expectations and see where it goes. Maybe there's a phone call you need to make that you've been putting off because you're not sure of the reaction you'll get. Don't *anticipate* the pain you might feel while making the call, just go and do it. Turn around and face whatever it is that's got you scared right now. Shine a light on the shadowy flickers of this fear and bring it into view. The more fully you can see the picture, the less fearful you'll be.

Think of one thing that is giving you anxiety right now, or something that has surpassed anxiety into the realm of real fear. Can you choose to stop running from it? And if you can be brave enough to stop, can you also be strong enough to turn around and face that fear? Don't think about whether it will be easy or not. That added anticipation will only add resistance to the situation. Just be curious, turn around, and look at what it is that's been causing you all of this pain. You may find that once you can see the whole picture, it's a lot less scary than you imagined.

Reflection

Forgiveness

Forgiveness is a gift to yourself

The act of forgiveness is considered showing mercy, especially to someone else, no matter if they asked for it or deserve it. It helps you find closure to a situation and move on, rather than carrying it with you. The unfortunate news is that unlike grief, there is no "one size fits all" common process for forgiveness; it's something that requires unique navigation for each situation.

Since it's a pretty heavy concept, let me tell you a funny story. As a teen, when I had to forgive people, I'd often think of the Bible verse that says to forgive someone "seventy times seven" times. At one point I decided to keep a physical ledger of how many times I'd forgiven people and the various offenses I'd forgiven them for, counting down to the moment when they no longer deserved that forgiveness. Then I grew up and realized the little math equation was just making the point that we are supposed to continue forgiving people, not actually keep a tally of how many times we've been wronged.

In many cases, people don't know or (unfortunately) don't care that they've hurt us. Carrying a torch in the hopes of receiving an apology that may never come is actually just burdening ourselves. The good news is that you have the choice to quietly forgive someone whenever you want and move on. You don't even have to tell the other party you've done it. You just make the decision and unshackle yourself from the burden of hurt they've placed on you.

And please, remember to extend forgiveness to yourself as well. We are often harder on ourselves than we are on anyone else. If you struggle with this, remind yourself that whatever it is you think you did wrong, you were just acting based on the knowledge you had at that time. There are hundreds of things I've said during my life that at the time I thought were very smart and well-reasoned, but looking back through my current lens of experience, I cringe so hard that my entire body tenses. But then I remind myself that in the vast majority of those cases, I truly didn't know any better and where possible, I've made amends. Sometimes all it takes to move on from our mistakes is the simple act of forgiving ourselves.

I do want to acknowledge that in some cases it can feel hard, if not impossible, to forgive someone for something they've done to you, especially in cases where your personal sovereignty may have been violated. Every situation is different and the pain from some experiences may never fully go away. In moments like this, I try to make forgiveness an offering to my future self. Even though the thought of forgiveness may feel insurmountable to me in the present, I know I don't want to feel that weight in the future, so I offer forgiveness in the hope of creating an easier path for myself later on.

Forgiveness is hard. Give yourself a ton of credit for even considering it, especially if it's something you struggle with. Can you find just one thing you can forgive someone or yourself for? It could be someone who cut you off in traffic, or someone who interrupted you during a meeting and made you feel small, or maybe your friend said something hurtful. Whatever it is, choose something easy to start with and quietly forgive. Practicing these little acts of forgiveness will make it easier when you encounter larger offenses.

Reflection

Fun

Have fun; it's the most important part

I don't know about you, but I struggle to "have fun." I went to a college prep school, so learning was more about grades and getting into a good college more than it was about enjoying the process. Sports were more about competition than they were about having a good time. Most of the things I spend my free time doing are geared towards output instead of delighting in the journey.

Just being alive means we have to do all kinds of not-fun things like going to the DMV, waking up early, running errands, doing dishes every single day for the rest of our lives. I'm sure you can come up with your own personal list. And the issues we regularly come across have health impacts on us. The American Psychological Association published a survey that found 76% of respondents have health issues from daily stressors like politics and inflation.[29] They report having "headaches, fatigue, depression, nervousness and exhaustion." 76%... That's over 3/4 of people who are physically affected in a negative way. That's pretty concerning.

But there is something that can help with these feelings: fun!

---

[29] Fulton, April. "Here's Why You Should Make a Habit of Having More Fun." *NPR*, NPR, 4 Feb. 2023, www.npr.org/sections/health-shots/2023/02/04/1150518287/fun-play-happiness-stress-reduction.

If we aren't mindful of how much fun we're having, then we might not have any at all. And what's the point of everything else if we can't enjoy ourselves?

I often think of what my brother told me while he was teaching me to golf. I tend to be tense, mentally running through the checklist of body parts being in place before a swing. Then he gently told me, "Remember, you're having fun. This is fun." Now when I'm golfing, if something is off, I reset and remind myself, "Natalie, remember, you're having fun." I instantly lighten up and get my swing back.

It's equal parts funny and embarrassing how often (daily) I have to tell myself, "Natalie, have fun. This is fun. You're having a good time." But without that reminder from myself, I too easily slip back into overachieving, perfectionist, competitive mode.

I once had a pencil case that was a gift from a friend, and it read, "It is not fun, why do it?" I'm not sure if the grammar was intentional, but it adds to the silliness of the statement and never fails to make me smile. Sometimes if I feel myself tensing up while working, I'll stop and ask myself," It is not fun, why do it?" At the very least, it makes me laugh a little.

No one was put on this Earth to spend our time chasing things that don't bring us joy. Perfection is a myth, because what's perfect to one person might not be to another. Winning trophies and awards is cool, but does it matter if you didn't enjoy the journey; if you still feel stressed and wanting?

So, how can we disengage from our achieving, compliant, competitive natures and tap into what we individually think is fun? The answer will be different for everyone, but here are a few ideas:

1. Laughter: I've written about the importance of laughter later on, but it's the simplest way to enhance your mood. I'm not really one for a belly laugh, but whenever I let myself actually express how funny I think something is, I feel instant lightness.

2. Self-talk: You can try the tactic of reminding yourself you're having fun when you feel tension creep in. If you're de-stressing with a coloring book and go outside the lines… oh well! There's no coloring book contest you're going to lose. Remind yourself you're doing the activity purely for fun.

3. Try something new: Learning new stuff can help take away the pressure to achieve. So what if you're not Picasso? You can follow along with a Bob Ross episode and still have a chill, good time. And learning new skills also helps the health of the gray matter in your brain.[30]

4. Play: just go play something. Anything. A video game. A pick-up game in the park. Trivia night at the bar. Solitaire with an actual deck of cards. Go play something where there are no stakes other than having a good time.

5. Gamify: Sometimes we have to do things we don't want to. That's a fact. So figure out how you can turn it into a game. Lots of apps exist to gamify the most mundane thing, like making your bed

---

[30] "Grey Matter." *Cleveland Clinic*, 19 Dec. 2024, my.clevelandclinic.org/health/body/24831-grey-matter.

in the morning or drinking enough water. And people pay for them! So make a free version for yourself or pay for one someone else has already made and add some fun to the game of life.

6. Be silly: One of my mom's most endearing qualities was that she was silly. If her grandkids didn't want to eat their vegetables, she'd put sprinkles on them. Whatever you have to do that is so not-fun that it's dragging you down, find a way to put some sprinkles on it.

The next time you notice that all of the fun is sucked out of what you're doing, stop and think of a way to change that up. Imagine what your day might look like if you made a conscious choice to have fun just 1% more of the time. Over time, if you practice making fun a part of your routine, then over time you'll start to enjoy yourself more and more, no matter what you're doing.

Reflection

Gentleness

Being gentle can support your biggest breakthroughs

Throughout my life, I've found it difficult to be gentle. I have a very straightforward nature and tend to jump right in after I have a plan. But as I've gotten older, I've realized how important it is to find gentleness in life.

So, I did some research to find out if it was just me who needed to find more gentleness, or if it was something everyone could benefit from, and it turns out, as it often does, many of us are in this boat together.

The biggest gift gentleness gives us is that it allows us to slow down. We are barreling from one activity to the next, stuck in traffic, missing out on sleep, sacrificing doing the activities we love. If we were to approach life in a gentle way, we couldn't help but slow down.

I learned this lesson when I recently broke my ankle. Every single thing required all of my attention to make sure I wasn't banging my ankle on anything or accidentally touching it on the floor. And after that, I had to re-learn to walk which required me to consciously remind my brain that even though it hurt to take a step, I was safe and I needed to do this. Being gentle was my only option in order to heal.

Along those lines, gentleness teaches us to be present. It is almost impossible to be gentle with a person in a situation if you're mentally rushing to think about what you're going to do or say in the future. Gentleness requires you to be in the moment so you can react as the situation unfolds. When a child holds their newborn sibling, what do parents always say? "Gentle! Be gentle with them!" Or if you've never been around a baby, think about something else, like a Jenga tower. No one wins Jenga by being haphazard. The most successful players are gentle with their moves, even if it's a move that requires a quick motion, like popping out a piece, but it's planned slowly, with finesse.

Gentleness helps us determine what's really important in our lives. Think about your day today (or yesterday if you're reading this in the morning). How much of what you wanted to do did you have to sacrifice because of the hustle and bustle of life? Now, replay the day and find some moments where you could have inserted some gentleness. Chances are you can find one or two places where you could have moved more slowly, mindfully, and gently through a situation.

Finally, gentleness just feels good. When you go to a spa, you aren't expecting to be treated roughly, having a robe shoved at you and being told to hurry up. You are there to relax, and a calm, gentle atmosphere helps you achieve that. When you start practicing gentleness, it signals to yourself and those around you that you care for them and that you are engaged in the current situation.

It's such a simple trait that we rarely think about, but that's why gentleness deserved its own chapter because I truly believe if we were all just 1% more gentle with ourselves and each other, this world would be a better place to live in. Can you find a time today to be 1% more gentle? Whether you're stuck behind a slow walker, doing a menial task you don't love, or just trying to get out of bed, how can you find gentleness?

Reflection

Goals

Shoot for the stars

I love setting goals for myself. Like, really ambitious goals that have a better chance of failing than being achieved. I feel if I fail at an ambitious goal, I make more progress trying to achieve it than if I'd set a lesser goal for myself.

For example, every year I set the goal to get my mind and body in shape to run a half marathon. I don't always sign up for an official half, but I like the challenge of knowing I can run 13.1 miles if I want. Most years, I get up to a 10-mile run and decide that's enough. Others, I run the full half. But either way, setting that 16 week training goal for myself gets me closer to running a half marathon than if I chose to only run a 5k or a 10k (both of which are great goals, too!).

You know what happens if you set a goal and you don't reach it? Nothing. You just take what lessons you can and keep going. Don't be afraid to set hard goals for yourself. It's okay not to reach them.

But if you never set a hard goal for yourself because you're scared of failing or that it will be too difficult, you'll never come close to reaching it either.

Consider a person who sets out to play the perfect level of a video game. They play the level over and over and over until they know all of the moves, all of the tricks, and all of the timing. They didn't give up after their first attempt and say, "Well, that's it. I failed." They kept trying. If you want to start a new habit but forget to do it one day, you don't throw your hands in the air and decide never to do it again. You just keep at it.

Your goals can be the same. Set a goal that you consider to be ambitious; something that's going to require some effort but not so much effort that you quit right at the start. Give yourself permission to not reach it. Strive to, but don't beat yourself up about it if you don't fully achieve it. Not only will this help you work hard towards your goal, it'll help you cultivate a more forgiving relationship with yourself.

There are lots of different methods for pursuing goals, and among the most popular is the S.M.A.R.T method. The acronym stands for Specific, Measurable, Achievable, Relevant, and Time-bound. Be specific about what your goal is so that you can work directly towards it. If possible attach some kind of metric to it, like tracking incremental progress so that you can make it measurable. Achievable is something we've already talked about a little, but "achievable" is going to be unique to you based on what you consider "achievable" to be. Your goal should be relevant to how you want your life to look, or the person you want to be. Time-bound means giving yourself a deadline to complete the goal.

Can you set one goal for yourself that will challenge you and make you feel good? If you need some structure to achieve it, take some time to map out the S.M.A.R.T. components so that you can keep yourself on track. Even if you just complete one goal, or part of one goal, you'll be better off than if you never started at all.

Reflection

Gratitude

It can come from unlikely places

I wasn't sure if I'd write about gratitude despite it being a popular topic. I'm by nature a very grateful person. The second I'm consciously awake, I take a few moments to be thankful for a warm cozy bed and a safe place to sleep. When everything feels like it's falling apart, I stop and express gratitude for something as small as clean drinking water. Even my signature on the original 1% Better newsletters ("With gratitude") was intentional because I'm always grateful anyone would take the time to read what's on my heart.

But that said, I never feel like the practice of gratitude "shifts my mindset" or relieves my anxiety. No matter how many times I read that anxiety and gratitude cannot coexist and that gratitude stops anxiety, I raise my eyebrows. I have definitely been grateful and anxious at the same time. When I lay in bed feeling grateful for being cozy, I'm also feeling anxious about everything else that needs to happen the second my feet hit the floor and the day gets going.

Then one of my sisters sent me an article. I'll confess, I almost didn't click it when I saw the headline, but if someone takes time and effort to show me something, I make the time to check it out. And she's my sister — duh, of course I'm clicking it.

It's an article explaining the wonderful science of gratitude, but what stood out to me most was this:[31]

"Gratitude helps people realize that they wouldn't be where they are without the help of others."

It stopped me in my tracks because I'd never heard gratitude expressed that way. Gratitude is frequently framed as this thing that is individual. What are *you* grateful for?

But when I read that quote, it highlighted how gratitude is about connection. It's actually not about us as individuals at all. It's about all of us together.

So when I express my gratitude as I'm lying in bed, I'm also expressing gratitude for all of the things that made this moment possible. The hands that made the bed, mattress, sheets, the companies that delivered these pieces, the job I have that afforded me the bed. The list can go on and on. And while my anxiety doesn't instantly dissipate, the more I move through my morning and my day, I can take in all of the people making my life what it is.

We don't do this — living life — in a vacuum. We do it together, in one way or another. We depend on each other, on people who for the most part we won't even know exist. It reminds us that even though we may be having individual experiences, we truly are supported by other people, many of whom we won't ever meet or know exist. Gratitude may start as something that is in your head

---

[31] Pratt, Misty. "The Science of Gratitude." *Mindful,* 13 Jan. 2025, www.mindful.org/the-science-of-gratitude/.

and your heart, but it's creating an energy that extends far beyond you, out to those who cross your path in one way or another.

Can you combat anxiety, negativity, and pain by being grateful for one thing today? Life can feel hard and sometimes hopeless, but remember there are millions of people out there who are connected with you, and you with them. You are important in ways which you may never know, and there are people who are grateful for you right this very moment.

Reflection

Grief

Grief is incomparable

Grief is a tough topic to write about because while I have a lot of personal experience with it, one thing I've learned is that no one is an expert in my grief; everyone's grief is unique and unpredictable. You can be in a room full of people who are all there to share your grief but you may feel only loneliness. That's because grief is a road that you have to walk alone. You can have support, but no one else experiences your exact feelings at the same times you do.

I remember shortly after my mom died, it was a hot day and I was swimming at the gym. Mid-lap, I remembered my mom teaching me how to swim and couldn't wait to text her that I'd made the time to go that day. But then I remembered I couldn't text her, and just like that, I was sobbing through the rest of my swim.

This is what grief does. It can be persistent and comes out of nowhere.

But like with all other emotions we have, we can make friends with grief. I don't mean wallowing in it, but instead of pushing it away, acknowledge it. I was 11 years old when my aunt and five cousins died in a car accident. When I missed them, my parents would take me to go get Jack-in-the-Box tacos (my aunt's favorite fast food) or I'd play some Fleetwood Mac because we always danced around to it when I visited them. Over time, by doing things they loved when, I turned my grief into something that made me smile.

That might not work for you, but the more you acknowledge your grief the more you find ways to handle it in healthy ways.

But let me back up a bit. First, I want to explain that grief isn't only related to death, and you can't compare your processing to how other people process.

There are lots of examples of non-death loss, which can include:
- Loss of health
- Loss of possessions
- Loss of a job
- Infertility
- Estrangement
- Relationship breakup

We may not think it's appropriate to "grieve" these things, but they are losses. Give yourself permission to acknowledge what someone or something meant to you instead of denying it.

When we learn of a loss, our body goes into fight, flight, or freeze for up to two days.[32] So when you remember that loss out of nowhere (like my incident in the pool), it can set off your nervous system again. There are different stages of grief (some say five stages, some say seven stages) but it's important to know they're

---

[32] Arthur, Amy. "Why Grief Is so Painful – and Critical to the Human Race." *BBC Science Focus Magazine*, 12 July 2023, www.sciencefocus.com/the-human-body/why-is-grief-so-painful.

not linear. So if you move past denial and then right back into it, that's okay.

Sometimes it's harder to see someone we care about going through the grieving process than it is to go through it ourselves because it's so personal that it leaves us feeling helpless. And since it's different for every individual, there's no "proven" way to go about being a part of their support system. But in researching healthy ways to be there for someone who is grieving, there are a few big themes.

Here are four tips for how to support someone who is grieving:

The biggest mistake people make is not reaching out or choosing to say nothing. Even though the person grieving might not be in a place to talk, it's still important that you voice your support for them. Send them a text, a DM, a voice memo, a card. Not everyone likes to talk on the phone but there are TONS of ways to reach out and let them know you're thinking about them.

Another tip is to be specific. Oftentimes we say, "Let me know if there's anything I can do." Well, as anyone who has been in the throes of grief knows, *they* may not even know what they need. Take it upon yourself to bring food, do some errands, offer to come clean the house; get creative! You know your friend or family member best, so you know what they'd likely need done. In my mom's final days, her friend came over every day. The first time she said, "No one was answering their phones and I wasn't sure what to do so I just came over." I have told her many times since then that I remain so grateful she showed up because I had no idea what we needed and she helped by simply being a steady presence.

Don't avoid talking about the loss, especially if it's a person or pet who has passed. Ask about some fun memories or something else that allows them to shine a light where there currently is only sadness. It may still hurt, but giving them the opportunity will be key to facing the loss over time. Especially if it's non-death grief, like the loss of a relationship or job, then talking about it will help dampen any shame that might be attached to it.

The most important thing you can do is listen. It's unhelpful to say things like, "You're going to be fine" when it may feel like their world is crumbling. Instead, ask how the person feels or just give them space to talk about whatever they want to. I love this tweet that went viral where someone was talking to their boyfriend and he asked, "Are you processing or looking for solutions?" This simple question helps set the stage and also lets the person know that you're truly there to support them in whatever way they need.

I'll admit that things can get tricky when other people are grieving the same loss as you because everyone grieves differently. So while you need to take care of yourself, give others a little grace for how they are responding as well. Some people like to commiserate together and others like to keep to themselves. Both are fine.

Supporting someone who is grieving all comes down to listening and accepting that you're not going to "solve" their grief for them.

The very best way to express love and support is by showing up and being there, and letting them feel whatever it is they're feeling.

If you are experiencing grief right now, can you take a moment to give yourself permission to feel it instead of pushing it down? Can you give yourself grace to know that grief lasts for however long it lasts and there's no finish line? Can you find ways to move forward? Can you share your struggle with someone if that will make you feel less alone? Can you avoid idealizing the past and dwelling on what-ifs? Can you tell yourself there's no guilt in having "good days"? If you're not dealing with grief right now, think back to times you did and what healthy coping mechanisms you used to get through it. Put those in your "emotional toolbox" should you ever need them when that fight-or-flight kicks in.

Reflection

Growth

"You've changed."

One time, a family member and I were discussing a topic we disagreed on. He said, "You've changed." For a while that bothered me because he said it to convey disapproval of my opinion. But then I realized that while it was meant to chastise me, it was actually a compliment!

Can you imagine if we were all the same person we were at 16 years old? 21 years old? 30 years old? As we age, we mature. We change. We learn new things and have new experiences which all shape us and the people we become.

That is called growth! And growth is a good thing. Even if you feel like you grew in the wrong direction for a while, you learned what you needed to do and now you're on another course.

I always like to dig into the science on various topics, but as one study notes, "there is a dearth of theory on [personal growth] as a process." So basically, even though there are thousands of books on the subject, very few studies have looked into how to achieve personal growth.[33] There are some trends they've identified though:

- Growth-related goals
- Narration of the life-story from a growth perspective

---

[33] Maurer, Mia, et al. "What Is the Process of Personal Growth? Introducing the Personal Growth Process Model." *New Ideas in Psychology*, Pergamon, 28 Apr. 2023, www.sciencedirect.com/science/article/pii/S0732118X2300017X.

- The growth mindset
- Striving towards meaningful goals with grit
- The motivation to grow
- Satisfaction of basic psychological needs

The paper continues, "These studies have been fundamental to deepening our understanding of this complex phenomenon and its related factors; they do not, however, explain it is an ongoing psychological process with distinct supportive conditions and subprocesses."

Ok, that's a lot of jargon so how does it apply to us? It means that personal growth is *PERSONAL*. It will look different for you than it will for someone else. It's also not linear.

There is no blueprint for how to grow and what that looks like for you. Some people act like they're in high school for their entire lives, while others continue to grow and mature. Either is fine, because it's all an individual and personal process. What is good for one person isn't the rule for everyone.

This is great news for those of us who struggle with comparison. If you feel like you're "behind" in life, or should be doing something different, stop worrying about it. You are growing exactly like you're supposed to. Plants are a great example of this. It's commonly unadvised to grow a rosemary plant from the seed because it takes much longer than growing it from a cutting, and once it starts to grow, it *grows*. One little asparagus shoot takes about three years to harvest! Meanwhile, you can plant a tomato seed and have a delicious homemade salsa in a matter of months.

Some plants grow tall while others of the same species stay short. All of them are perfect in their own way, and more importantly, they can't be rushed.

Think about your own personal growth. How can you give yourself 1% more support in your journey without putting unnecessary pressure on yourself? Give yourself credit for continuing to grow and change even under less than perfect conditions. Be open to the concept of growth. Be open to the idea that who you are today is not your final form. How can you learn from where you're at right now? And be kind to those who are walking their own path as well. Maybe they aren't doing things the way you think they should, but that's okay. Let them grow at their own pace and in their own way.

Reflection

Guilt

Guilt is all in your head, literally

Guilt is a pretty terrible feeling. Sometimes, people can experience such deep guilt that they carry it around with them for their entire lives. But we can unpack guilt and start freeing you from the grip it has on your life.

Guilt and shame are closely linked, but they are not the same thing, so there is a chapter on shame later on as well. For now, we're going to talk about guilt, how it impacts us, and how to take the power back from it.

What is guilt? Guilt is a more personal emotion than shame because it's internally motivated. Feelings of guilt arise because of our own preconceived notions of what is right and wrong. That is why someone who is a chronic dieter might feel guilty about eating an entire pint of ice cream in one sitting, whereas someone who has no feelings one way or the other about dieting won't think twice about pounding that pint. One person has a preconceived notion about what amount of ice cream is appropriate and the other doesn't. It's as simple as that.

Guilt is triggered by our own actions or inactions and how they align with what we believe. Think about parents who lament the things they should and shouldn't have done with their kids, like spending more time with them, going to more of their games, or trying to be a part of their lives in some other way. These feelings are internally motivated, and cause the parent guilt even if the child didn't feel wronged at all.

This is why guilt is different for everyone, because we all have different feelings and priorities. Guilty is a deeply personal, deeply individual experience.

Spending too much time feeling guilty can not only make us feel bad for the moment, but it can construct a negative self-image and potentially send us into a spiral that only results in us doing more things that make us feel guilty. This is part of what makes recovery for addiction so tough. Feeling those moments of guilt and shame makes people want to escape, sending them right back to the substance or behavior that caused the problem in the first place.

Maybe you've been in a situation where someone tried to convince you that you'd done something wrong even though you truly didn't feel like you did. But the more they explained it, the more you started to believe it until you felt guilty about something you weren't even aware of before. This is another tricky and complex social piece of guilt. It's where the idea of gaslighting comes into play. You did nothing wrong, but someone shames you and makes you feel like you did. So now, you have this new belief about what is right and what is wrong and it's causing you guilt.

How can you tame your guilt?

First, accept that you can't change the past. What's done is done and all that you have is the present moment. Take a few deep breaths acknowledging the loss of time, opportunity, or whatever it is causing you guilt. On your exhales, envision yourself letting that guilt go. On your inhales, imagine the freedom you have in this moment to do something you feel good about.

Second, forgive yourself. Now that you've emptied your cup of these guilty feelings, you're able to focus on reminding yourself that it's okay, that you're just a human who is trying to balance all of the obligations of life, the dreams you have for yourself, and the constraints of time and energy. If you made a rash decision, did something out of character, or in some other way "messed up," just forgive yourself over and over until it sticks. It may take some time, but eventually, with consistency, you will forgive yourself.

Third, know who you are and what you believe in. Are you carrying around guilt because of an idea that someone else put into your head or do you actually think that something is wrong? What are your own core beliefs about what is true and moral? We sometimes hear the phrase "moral gray area" and that applies here. If you know to your core who you are and what you believe, then there will be less and less opportunities for you to feel guilt. Nothing can make you feel guilty if you know what you believe to be true. You may do something that someone else disagrees with, but in the end, you made the choice because of your own moral compass and that's what's most important.

Fourth, make a plan to stop feeling guilt. If you missed your child's soccer game, try to plan ahead so you can make the next one. Or if you really don't care about going and someone else is making you feel bad about it, then learn how to address that within yourself. If you feel guilty for spending money on getting takeout food often, make it a point to have food you look forward to eating at home. Whatever is making you feel guilt, know deep within that you have the power to relieve it.

Think about what triggers guilt for you, or if you have a specific past moment in mind, explore what it is about that moment that made you feel guilty. Can you reflect on if it actually aligns to your personal values or if it was imprinted on you by someone else? Can you come up with a plan to relieve just 1% more of your guilt? It can be simply reminding yourself that you actually *don't* feel guilt over something or making a plan to change your behavior. Whatever it is, you'll be on your way to being free from guilt.

Reflection

Habits

You are always making habits

Whether you realize it or not, you are always in the process of making habits. And over time, your conscious habits become automatic actions that you take whether you realize it or not. What once started as an intention to make a habit has now turned into something you do without thinking about it.

But that can be a double-edged sword because when you intend to do something and choose not to, then that choice becomes the new habit. For example, if you want to make it a habit to get up and workout in the morning, every time you choose to hit the snooze button instead, you are now reinforcing that the snooze button is the new habit. When you want a snack and mindlessly eat something while you're staring into the fridge, you are making that action a habit without thinking about it. This is why understanding habits is so important, because they are going to be part of our lives whether we think about it or not.

There's general guidance that it can take anywhere from 21 days up to 254 days to make a habit stick. The European Journal of Social Psychology says that 66 days is the magic number to turn the habit into an automatic behavior.[34]

---

[34] Solis-Moreira, J. (2024, February 20). *How long does it really take to form a habit?*. Scientific American. https://www.scientificamerican.com/article/how-long-does-it-really-take-to-form-a-habit/

The idea is that eventually, your habits become so second nature that you don't even need motivation to make them happen.

So, how do you start developing healthy habits? The good news is there are lots of strategies, including simply reminding yourself why you're doing the action in the first place. Personally, the way to create habits that's been most helpful is called habit stacking. This is when you connect one habit to another that helps you remember to do it until it becomes second nature. That's how I finally made flossing a no-brainer. I was already brushing my teeth at night so I stacked my flossing onto the automatic behavior. If you're a person who loves checking items off a "to do list," try making a chart for 66 days, 100 days, or however long you think you need to make a habit, and then check it off each day. Habit tracking apps that can also help gamify the process for you so that you can get little rewards and dopamine hits to keep you going.

There are all kinds of tactics for making new habits, so experiment with them to find out what will work best for you. And keep in mind that no matter what, you are always reinforcing some kind of behavior to your brain, so try to make it one you are pleased with.

Choose one new behavior that you want to bring into your life and choose a plan of action to help it stick. Don't start with a ton at once because that might be overwhelming and set yourself up for failure. So, just start with one, give it all of your mental support, and see what happens.

Reflection

Healing

Give yourself grace and space

When I started thinking about the concept of healing, I realized the myriad ways we can hurt. Our bodies can hurt, our feelings can hurt, our brains can make us think we're hurt as a form of self-preservation. It's actually kind of a miracle that there are ever moments when we feel fully un-hurt.

I know I'm not alone in being bad at letting myself have the time I need to heal from things. I want to get back to living, to move around, to feel normal. But often I end up hurting myself even more when I don't take the time I need to rest and heal.

I find that another annoying part of healing is that everyone heals differently. There is no benchmark specific to you. Because we have different bodies, different lives, different everything. Even identical twins haven't had identical lived experiences, haven't felt the same emotions, etc.

We are all different. So what one person needs is very obviously and understandably going to be different from you. It may even be different from past versions of yourself! 37yo Natalie is NOT doing a great job at accepting that she heals from injury a lot slower than 27yo Natalie did, but those are the facts.

So I'm constantly reminding myself not to rush the process. It's not going to help anything. Our bodies are trying their hardest to execute a slow process while also being bombarded by the necessity of movement, the strain of mental stress, and the pressure to be socially available to friends, family, and colleagues.

Listen to your physical body, your subtle body, and your inner workings that make you human. You will let yourself know when you're ready, when you're healed. Surgeries may take longer to heal than we'd like. Maybe your body has changed and you simply can't do the things you once could. Accepting that also takes some mental healing to come to grips with the fact that your situation has changed.

The Greek physician Hippocrates said, "Healing is a matter of time, but it is sometimes also a matter of opportunity." What would it look like if you created the opportunities for yourself to heal? If you noticed that you need time, space, rest, or whatever else you require to heal?

Meet yourself wherever you're at in your healing journey for whatever it is you're healing from. If you need space from people, take it. If you need to skip going for a run to let your body rest, do it. If you need to cry, do it. Look for ways to give yourself the opportunity to heal and to show yourself grace.

Reflection

Idling

Resisting the urge to do more

As a chronic overachiever and a naturally curious person, I am always doing something. I'm always in some kind of course or working on several projects at once. So for me, when I do my nightly evaluation of, "Was I 1% better today?" sometimes the answer is no for an unexpected reason: I pushed myself too hard. After many years of working 12-hour days early in my career, I've had to break myself of thinking compulsive working is the answer to everything. Bored? Why not work a little. Need some money? Pick up a couple of freelance jobs. Projects not performing well? Work harder on SEO and SEM.

But constantly going and grinding is not always the answer. Over the past few years, I've worked really hard on doing less. When I make the conscious decision to not give into the impulse to work, I find that my stress levels go down, I have more energy to do the activities that bring me joy, I create the space to discover new things that make me happy, and I'm not constantly teetering on the edge of burnout.

So if I've had one of those busy days where my anxiety compels me to work non-stop, I know that at the end of the day I'm not a better person for giving in to that. The thing that would have been better for me would have been to rest.

Over time, I'm getting better at this. If I'm tired I rest instead of making another cup of coffee to get me through the next task. If I'm too tired for a vigorous workout I'd had planned, I do some yin yoga instead. The examples go on and on.

Sometimes the best thing you can do for yourself is nothing, not more. Can you identify 1% of your life where you could use a bit of idling?

Reflection

Imposter

And how to release yourself from it

For those who aren't familiar with the term, Imposter Syndrome is when people don't feel "good enough" or skilled enough for the positions they're in or for the accolades they've received. In fact, it is personal success that triggers Imposter Syndrome and about 70% of adults will experience it at some point in their lives.[35]

But I want to reframe this, starting with the idea of manifestation.

Posts and videos about manifesting are everywhere these days, and a consistent piece of advice people give is that you have to start embodying the life you want to lead.

For example, if you want to be more physically fit, then you have to lead your life in the way a physically fit person would. Or if you want to be a musician, you need to wake up and move through your day the way a musician would, picking up your instrument and playing "just because."

So, how does this relate to Imposter Syndrome?

You have the job you have, which means someone deemed you capable of doing it. Someone saw something in you that you may not be able to see in yourself. Or if you received some kind of recognition, it was because you deserved it even if you didn't think you did.

---

[35] "Imposter Syndrome." *Psychology Today,* Sussex Publishers, www.psychologytoday.com/us/basics/imposter-syndrome.

So if you're feeling like you are fooling everyone and can't do something, think about applying the practice of manifesting. Go through your day as though you already are the best at whatever it is you are feeling like you're an imposter. And understand that even the people who are the experts had to learn lessons along the way.

Still not convinced? Let me tell you a little secret…

EVERYONE is pretending at first. Everyone.

No one knows how to *do* something until they *have* to do something. Take parents for example. Parents can read tons of Parenting books. And do you know what happens once they are parents? They say, "This wasn't covered in the book."

Every surgeon has a "first day." What if you're the patient on that surgeon's first day? Do you want a surgeon who thinks, "What am I DOING here?!" or the surgeon who thinks, "Shut up, Brain. I've got this."

You've got this, too!

Writing this book, I had to shove down the imposter a ton of times. Who do I think I am giving people advice? Then I reminded myself of all of the reasons why I started writing the original newsletter, and all of the people who reached out to tell me it helped them, and I remember that even though I may feel insecure at times, if this book helps even one person, then that's worth it!

You are not an imposter either. You are *EXACTLY* where you are meant to be right now. And if you weren't, you wouldn't be there.

The next time there's a little voice in your head saying you can't do something or another negative thought, take a moment to flip whatever that voice says into a positive. You can do anything you put your mind to.

Reflection

Increase

Release to increase

Sometimes I wonder if the concept of being 1% better is off-putting. We are all awesome just as we are this very second, so why do we need to be better if we're good enough? Then one day I heard an interview with NFL quarterback Jameis Winston. The nugget that stuck out to me was that Jamies kept talking about being "men of increase," or in other words, men who are constantly trying to increase their skills, their wellbeing, their relationships, all of it. Men of increase.

This idea has continued to surface for me. I'm at a time in my life where I'm trying not to stress about things that aren't actually important, which isn't easy. It's also hard for me to figure out how to be less Type A while also striving to be 1% better every day (which has been my goal ever since I read about the idea over a decade ago). Can you always be better while doing less?

Then it hit me: "Increase" isn't always more. Sometimes less is more. It's a simple and sometimes cliché saying but it's true. Our brains struggle to subtract instead choosing to build on the first idea we have and the subsequent ideas after that. When problem solving, we have one idea, then another, and try to figure out how the two can work together.

But sometimes to increase in anything, we need to first subtract. This is prevalent in many major religions where people are encouraged to give their troubles to a deity in order to make room for more of what they want in their lives.

Much of becoming a "person of increase" has to do with making room in our lives for that to happen. I started thinking about all of the possible areas of life where we can release to increase. Time management, relationships, spiritual wellbeing, finances, health, etc. The list goes on and, as always, will be different for everyone.

Coming back to the thought I opened this with: is it less stressful to reframe being 1% better as constantly increasing? Sometimes (though not always) the answer will be to first take stock of what really matters and what can be released.

How can you change the way you think of quantifying "being 1% better" every day? Can you release to increase your sense of peace, your time spent doing activities you enjoy? Can you increase in an area of your finances that you want to improve?

Reflection

Increments

Little increments add up to big changes

We live in a world of instant gratification, which makes it hard when we have to wait for something to happen. Everything is so instant that waiting has become an uncomfortable concept to many of us. But what if we thought about it in terms of increments instead of waiting?

Weight loss or weight gain is something almost everyone can relate to. Whether someone is trying to shed fat or put on muscle, sometimes it can feel like a slog waiting to see the results. So, what happens? They start to feel discouraged and give up. But what if every single pound was a reason to celebrate because in the end, all of those pounds stack up. If someone needed to lose 52 lbs, that might sound daunting until they realize it's just an increment of 1 lb per week. Over a year's time, that 52 lbs is done and dusted. Or what if someone wanted to save money? Putting away $20/week, or $2.75/day, over the course of a year would amount to just over $1,000 saved without much sacrifice

I think about this a lot when it comes to writing. If I write 500 words per day, that takes me about 30-45 minutes. It hardly seems like I'll be able to write a book with only that small amount, right? But if I continue stacking up those small increments, I'll have a

60,000 word book written in four months, which means I could write three books per year. How's that for progress?

No matter what we want to do, if we continually compare our current status to where we're supposed to go, it will start to seem like too great of a journey to get there and we'll give up. But if we think about the increments and take the time to celebrate the completion of each one, then we set ourselves up for success. After each increment is finished, we don't think, "I have so many more to go." Instead, we just acknowledge that it's one more down.

After a rough day, my friend and I jokingly text each other, "One day closer to retirement," and it immediately puts a positive spin on it. No matter what happened that day, it's over, and we can acknowledge that we got through it, and can move on. No matter what it is you want to accomplish, even if it's just a little small tweak in your daily life or habits, count your increments, not how far you have to go.

Even the concept of this book is built on the idea of increments. If you can consciously be just 1% better every day, over the course of a lifetime, that stacks up in unimaginably positive and fruitful ways. It's easy to do one thing that will move you closer to the person you want to be and the life you want to have.

Can you identify areas of your life where you're getting discouraged by the progress (or lack of it) and give yourself credit for the increments you made today towards your goal? Can you make it a point to celebrate the completion of those little increments and not fixate on the more negative angle about how far away the end of the goal is? Over time, even this small tweak in your mindset will add up and soon you'll start celebrating the increments and enjoying the journey.

Reflection

Inner child

Let the magic out

I have a theory that part of what people love about decorating for the holidays is it's a chance for us as adults to let out our inner child. We get to assemble our little Christmas villages, put train tracks around the base of the tree, cover everything in lights and ornaments, and bake sugary treats. Playing make believe, being creative, and giving into the urge for sugar. Who didn't love these activities as a kid?

Whether you were a child who was encouraged to express yourself or a child who was stifled, there's good news: you can still engage with and heal your inner child as an adult. In one study, they took a look at older people and how their inner child affects their lives.[36] It found that those who incorporated the childlike things they enjoy had an easier time turning negative experiences into positive ones.

We all need a sense of wonder in our lives.

So, how do you work on getting to know your inner child? Start by asking yourself, "What did Little Me do when I had nothing but time? What did I *want* to do?"

---

[36] Sjöblom, Margareta, et al. "Health throughout the Lifespan: The Phenomenon of the Inner Child Reflected in Events during Childhood Experienced by Older Persons." *International Journal of Qualitative Studies on Health and Well-Being*, U.S. National Library of Medicine, 16 June 2016, pmc.ncbi.nlm.nih.gov/articles/PMC4912602/.

This answer may not come easily. I've always been a pretty serious person. I'm quick to joke, but in my own head, I spend a lot of time thinking and contemplating. So a few days passed before the revelations started coming to me. For the life of me, I couldn't picture Little Natalie having fun. I've always tended to do things with an objective in mind, which inherently strips some of the fun out of it. But after giving myself the time to mull it over, I had an arsenal of ideas. Now, I try to incorporate some of that into my life every day to make sure I'm showing up for my inner child.

Go out and explore what makes you happy. If you loved playing with your friends as a child, find opportunities to hang out and be silly with friends. Find one area of your house that you can decorate however you want, if that's something that will bring you joy. You can try a wild new recipe using ingredients you often consider "off limits." You can experiment with a new craft or hobby.

The key is to give yourself permission to do this stuff without judgment. So what if other people don't enjoy the same activities as you? You didn't care about those opinions when you were young until someone called attention to it. I think we all have at least one memory of something we truly loved and thought was so special, only to have it ridiculed by someone else, tarnishing the shine for ourselves.

Tap into your inner child 1% more often and create an inner judgment-free zone to let your imagination run wild. If you need ideas, look around you. What seems fun? Try different activities to see what lights you up.

Reflection

Introspection

Go within yourself

How often are you curious about yourself? How often do you stop your thoughts and wonder, "Why did I just react like that?" Or "Why do I think this way about this subject?" Introspection is the act of examining our thoughts and feelings, and it's one of the most important but potentially hardest acts we can do.

We spend a lot of our time avoiding our feelings, or pushing down thoughts that we think are wrong or not worth our time. But it can be very beneficial for us. Studies show that it can lead to greater self-awareness, confidence, increased empathy, better leadership skills, and the ability to create a clearer self-concept.[37, 38] Who doesn't want those things?

To start an introspection process is simple, but to actually follow through can be hard because you may not like the stuff it brings up. It reminds me of something a friend said to me before my first therapy session, "Remember, you might find out that you're the one creating this situation. Are you ready for that?"

---

[37] Cherry, MSEd, K. (2023, April 4). *Introspection and how it is used in psychology research.* Verywell Mind. https://www.verywellmind.com/what-is-introspection-2795252

[38] Rose, Dr. H. (2022, August 18). *The power of introspection.* Ness Labs. https://nesslabs.com/introspection

If you could understand why you have a strong reaction to certain situations, how would that improve your life? I once experienced an incident that caused me to have PTSD. Out of nowhere, I'd see flashbacks and had no control over when they happened nor how I reacted. I'd black out and all I could see was the incident again. After tons of research, I stumbled on a tactic where I forced myself to remember the incident and journaled it in vivid detail. This was hard, but by doing it, I was signaling to my brain that the incident was just another thing that happened and it wasn't something I needed to push down. Often the things that we don't want to think about are the ones that pop up at the worst times. Hello, Intrusive Thoughts!

Think about something recently that left you feeling unsettled. Now ask yourself what was unsettling about it? Was it the way someone spoke to you? The tone of their voice? The content of their conversation? Or was it something you did that felt out of character? Investigate that feeling a little more.

We spend a lot of time thinking about all kinds of things, many of them unhelpful in terms of our personal growth. Can you spend just 1% more of your time investigating your feelings, emotions, and reactions to figure out the root of "why"? It doesn't have to be in the moment, it can be later. But give yourself the gift of the time and space to think through why something bothered you so much.

Reflection

Kindness

If you can be anything, be kind

I don't need to tell you that we are living through a very self-centered time in the world. It seems like everywhere you look, someone is trying to have the most controversial opinion, provoke people who are different from them, and generally sow discord so they can feed their own egos.

It is also clear that kindness rarely gets rewarded. But that's okay because kindness shouldn't be something we express in order to be seen, it should be something we do because it feels right to be kind to the beings we share this life with.

The world is noisy, and busy, and we're never doing enough nor are we doing things the right way, yada, yada, yada. It's very easy to get caught up in being hard on ourselves and, in turn, being hard on others. But I have found in these moments that one of the best ways to break this spiral is to simply do something kind.

As silly as it sounds, it seems that we have forgotten how easy it is to be kind. But it's easy to change that. Here are some fast and easy ways to cultivate kindness in your life today:

- Text a friend that you're thinking of them and you hope they have a nice day
- Let someone have a parking spot and go for one a little further away
- Do a loving kindness meditation

- Do a chore for someone or take something off their "to do" list
- Venmo a friend $5 for a coffee
- Tell a stranger you like their shirt

There are so many ways we can be kind to each other but we just don't think to do it. And that's understandable. There's a lot going on in the world, so it can be hard to add "be kind to someone" to your plate, but if you do it just a few times, kindness will become a habit and you won't even think about it anymore.

If you need more reason to be kind, there are piles of studies that show being kind makes us feel good. We may actually get more out of it than the people that we're being kind to. It releases oxytocin in our brains, it decreases anxiety and depression, it makes us feel more connected… the list goes on.

Today, think of one action you can take to show kindness to someone you know or maybe even a stranger. You can use some of the exercises mentioned above or you can come up with your own that feel right in the moment. The more it feels personal to you, the more likely you'll be to carry on the action until it becomes a habit.

Reflection

Laughter

It has amazing benefits

Do you know how many benefits we can get just from laughing? Studies show there are a lot, both short- and long-term. According to the Mayo Clinic, it will:

- Stimulate your organs
- Increase oxygen intake
- Release endorphins
- Reduce stress
- Ease tension
- Improve your immune system
- Ease pain by releasing the body's natural painkillers
- Improve your mood over the long term

Other studies show it can stimulate gamma brain waves — like in meditation — and increase mental clarity and creativity.[39]

All of that just from a little laughing.

This is something I work on a lot. It sounds silly to say I "work on laughing" but it's true. It's not that I don't like funny stuff or laughing out loud, but for some reason I just don't do it. When I think something is funny, I'll typically say, "That's funny!" with a

---

[39] Migala, Jessica. "Why Laughter Is so Good for You - and How to Do It More." *EverydayHealth.Com*, www.everydayhealth.com/self-care/how-to-laugh-more-every-single-day-why-its-so-good-for-you/.

smile. But one day a friend responded by asking, "Then why don't you laugh? If you think it's funny, laugh. Don't just say it's funny."

So, how can a person incorporate laughter into their life more?

One simple tip is to intentionally take 5-10 minute breaks for laughter or fun. Seek out short, funny video clips and let yourself laugh. Let those gamma waves take over. Or follow some comedians on social media so that you laugh a little while you scroll.

Go to a standup comedy show. There's evidence that laughing together in a group has a powerful effect on our wellbeing.

Write down "Three funny things" in a journal. This is like a journaling practice but different for obvious reasons. By the time you're done writing them down, you'll likely be laughing out loud. And as a bonus, this is a journal you'll actually may want to go back and read for a change.

Start to find 1% more ways to incorporate laughter into your life. All those benefits are too good to pass up when all you have to do to experience them is just laugh!

Reflection

Learning

Live longer by being a lifelong learner

Whether you loved school or hated it, the good news is there are still ways to become a lifelong learner. In fact, even if you think you hate learning, I bet there are some aspects of it that you love, and embracing learning can help your wellbeing in all kinds of ways. Let's dive in.

Start with the basics: School. Studies show that every year of schooling, including primary school, increases your longevity by 2%.[40] That means you can add years to your life simply by going to school. And it doesn't have to be anything crazy. You can go to a local junior college and take a class that interests you each semester, or commit to an online course. There are so many ways to reap the benefits of schooling later into your life.

But if you're not a fan of school, there are lots of practical options to make learning accessible. You can pick up a hobby or watch videos online to get better at an activity you already like. I'm an okay painter, but I love painting and I've always wanted to be really good at it, so this is something I'll commonly do on a weekend morning. Then I spend an hour or two painting, trying to flex that

---

[40] Leach-Kemon, K. (n.d.). *The longevity-boosting power of Education*. Institute for Health Metrics and Evaluation.
https://www.healthdata.org/news-events/insights-blog/acting-data/longevity-boosting-power-education

skill. Every now and then, there's nothing quite like following along with Bob Ross to make your soul feel good. If you're a more active person, you can try a new sport like pickleball and look for games at your local gym or community center.

Besides the fact that learning can increase your lifespan, it can also provide you with benefits right now. Learning new skills can help you get ahead in your job, whether they're skill-related or more geared towards increasing interpersonal talents, like more effective communication. And importantly, it can help you keep up with our ever-changing world. Think about how many AI programs are available right now and then multiply that out over the coming years. By being curious about how they work and playing with them, you can stay on top of the changing technology. I often think about what it would be like to be a person who was cryogenically frozen at the beginning of the 1980s and what their life would be like if they were unfrozen at this point in history. We may not have broad use of flying cars, but there would be a hugely significant learning curve for them to overcome just to understand the baseline technology of how our society functions.

Okay, you're sold on the importance of learning, but you just don't have the time for it. What can you do? You can start small!

Find a podcast about a topic you're interested in and listen to 20-30 minute episodes while you're in the car, the school pick-up line, doing the dishes, grocery shopping, etc. You can also break it up into smaller chunks if you need to do that.

Another way to start learning right now is to just get curious. If you see something and wonder, "How was that made?" or "How can I do that?" follow your curiosity down the rabbit hole. Look it up on YouTube or TikTok or wherever you like to find educational videos. The best part about this method is that you can find so much FREE content that you may learn everything you want to know without spending a dime.

Maybe you like books but don't have time to read them. Well, you can try an audiobook, also free using a library card. Or commit to reading just 10 pages each day. In a month, you'll have finished or be close to finishing an average-length book.

Whatever it is you like to do or are interested in, there's an opportunity to lean into that and start making learning a habit. Can you find a way to squeeze 1% more learning into your week? Finding just 20 minutes if you have a tight schedule to choose to do an activity that will enrich your brain and your life.

Reflection

Leisure

Explore the buckets of leisure

It seems like the older we get, we prioritize leisure less and less. And it also feels confusing because what is leisurely to one person may be your own personal hell. Some people like to decompress and relax on vacation while others want to squeeze in as many fun activities as possible. Both are great examples of leisure! But we need more leisure than just a few days of vacation each year. So, how can we all incorporate more leisure into our lives and why is it imperative to do so?

The science is simple, clear, and conclusive: leisure activities improve mental health.[41] There's a direct link between lack of leisure activities and mental health issues like anxiety, depression, and stress. So, if we want to feel better, incorporating more leisure is a good first step. And you don't even have to go on vacation to reach that relaxing state.

Part of the reason these activities make us feel better is that leisure = freedom.[42] And yes, those studies also show that wealthier

---

[41] Takiguchi, Yuta, et al. "The Relationship between Leisure Activities and Mental Health: The Impact of Resilience and Covid-19." *Applied Psychology. Health and Well-Being*, U.S. National Library of Medicine, Feb. 2023, pmc.ncbi.nlm.nih.gov/articles/PMC9538683/.

[42] Iso-Ahola, Seppo E., and Roy F. Baumeister. "Leisure and Meaning in Life." *Frontiers*, Frontiers, 1 Feb. 2023, www.frontiersin.org/journals/psychology/articles/10.3389/fpsyg.2023.1074649/full

people or business owners tend to have more leisure time because they make their own schedules. While we may not all live that life, we can incorporate the lessons of freedom into our own.

The first step is to look for opportunities in your schedule where you can offer yourself some of that openness, even if it's only for an hour or two. Once you've carved out the time for leisure, the next question for many people is, "What do I do now?"

It turns out there are specific types of leisure.[43] Generally, there are two main buckets: active and passive leisure, which are pretty self-explanatory. One involves doing something (like a hobby or playing a sport) the other is chilling (like watching a movie or reading a book). Those buckets are broken up further into social leisure, cognitive leisure, and physical leisure.

Social leisure is — you guessed it! — being social, doing activities with other people, going to concerts, traveling, etc.

Cognitive leisure is an activity that engages your brain, like learning a new language, reading a book, developing a new skill. This is a very nerdy confession, but one of my favorite cognitive leisure activities is to think of an obscure sports hypothesis and then spend an hour or two diving into the data to find a solution. To each their own!

---

[43] Akers, Alicia Sparks. "The 3 Types of Active Leisure (& How They Can Help Your Mental Health)." *Psych Central*, Psych Central, 19 June 2020, psychcentral.com/blog/your-mind/2020/06/the-3-types-of-active-leisure-how-they-can-help-your-mental-health.

Physical leisure is about getting your body moving, playing sports, etc. While running or hiking may be torture to some people, it's relaxing and leisurely to others.

This is where hobbies come into play.[44] They can fit into any of these buckets because they can involve as much or as little of these activities as you want. Hobbies can be anything from volunteering to photography to writing fanfiction. Which leads me to the fact I found most interesting…

Simply being a fan is a leisure activity![45] The act of fandom is an opportunity to engage in leisure. According to Psychology Today:

"Fans who participate in creating fanfiction or fan art, or who travel to fan conventions or concerts or football games, are engaging in what is known as serious leisure. This concept is based on the idea of involvement, a psychological trait defined as a state of motivation, arousal, or interest toward a recreational activity or associated product—anything from a television show to an actor to a basketball team."

If you're anything like me, you may be thinking, "Natalie, these are all things that take effort for me to do. How can that possibly help me de-stress?" Well, it turns out we may not know our brains as well as we think we do.

---

[44] Parkhurst, Emma. "How Hobbies Improve Mental Health." *USU*, 14 Dec. 2023, extension.usu.edu/mentalhealth/articles/how-hobbies-improve-mental-health.

[45] https://www.psychologytoday.com/us/blog/the-science-fandom/202109/why-leisure-is-never-waste-time

In the book "Stillness is the Key," author Ryan Holiday explains that leisure is one thing you can't do for anyone else; you have to do it for yourself. It "simultaneously relaxes and challenges us."

On the *Huberman Lab Podcast*, Dr. Andrew Huberman explains that a challenge, like trying a new pose in yoga, actually gives us a hit of dopamine because if we're off balance, we're learning something new in order to get back in balance.

So, yes, you're right that all of these activities require a degree of effort, even if it's just mentally engaging with what you're watching on your screen. But that effort is exactly what causes your brain to release dopamine — aka a "feel good hormone." Learning something new, trying to beat a video game, finishing a good book, they're all new experiences for your brain, and when your brain encounters that challenge and/or newness it feels good.

How can you make room for 1% more leisure in your life? How can you take control of your schedule 1% more in order to give your brain the break it needs and craves? And if you're not sure what you like to do for leisure, can you try one new activity in each of the social, cognitive, and physical leisure buckets? Explore what it is that lights up your brain while also making you feel good.

Reflection

Lessons

Everything can be an opportunity for growth

"I hope you've learned your lesson" is likely a phrase we're all familiar with, but unfortunately it's typically said in a negative tone. What if we thought about lessons in a positive light… because that's what lessons are!

Think about it: If you said, "I want to learn how to care less about what people think of me," and someone said, "Good news! You can buy this course for $100 and at the end, you'll free yourself from caring about what others think of you!" there's a good chance that you'd buy it. Well, that's what life offers us!

Everytime we do something and have a particular feeling about it — shame, anger, remorse, etc. — that's our free lesson that we can be thankful for. We have the opportunity to reframe the event and say, "Thank you for this feeling of regret, because now I know this isn't something I want in life," or "Thank you for this feeling of loss because it will help me to be more present with the people I have in my life."

Of course, it's natural to wallow in our feelings a bit, especially if they are familiar feelings. Our brains like what's familiar. The first time your brain encounters a feeling, it becomes familiar with that feeling and it will be easier for it to default to that feeling next time you're in a similar situation. It takes time, awareness, and effort to reframe them and rewire your brain in these instances. But it's worth it!

Imagine doing a presentation at work and absolutely crumbling while you're in the front of the room. Maybe you were asked unforeseen questions or your slides weren't as clear as you thought. It was a disaster. BUT it was also a treasure trove of lessons! You learned a new way to query your own content next time, you learned what people need in order to be clear on your message, and you learned how to handle your emotions both in the moment and afterwards.

Imagine how many other moments there are where we can flip the script and look at them as free lessons instead of reflecting poorly on ourselves.

So, how do we start to identify lessons in the moment?

For me, it always starts when I feel a strong emotion. I'm pretty mild mannered so if I get worked up about something, I know there's a lesson for me to dig into. In basketball, there's something called a "heat check" where players shoot the ball to see if their shots are still going in. These moments in our lives when we feel a strong emotion can be our own personal heat check. How are we dealing with particular situations when we are feeling deeply? Are we coping in a way that feels supportive to us? If not, what can we do to show ourselves compassion and support?

How can you reframe 1% more of your tough moments and decisions into a positive opportunity to learn a lesson? How can you use those experiences to better understand yourself, your desires, and your motivations?

Reflection

Mind-reading

It isn't just for fortune tellers

Whether you realize it or not, you're a mind-reader. Not in the "let me look into your future" sense, but in a psychological sense.

Imagine that you've just bumped into someone. You say "Sorry! Didn't see you there!" and the person responds with a chilly, "Yeah; it's fine," then walks away.

What is your brain doing? It's trying to read the response the person gave you. Was the person mad? Was the person mentally preoccupied and genuinely didn't care? You'll likely never know, but your brain will try to read the other person's mind and you'll form a story based on it.

It's the classic scenario of the "K" text. If you text someone back and they reply with "K," … oh buddy, are you in trouble. Or are you? It's totally normal for people who aren't as text savvy or just don't like texting to keep messages to a minimum and just say "K" as an acknowledgement. But we can't stop our brains from trying to mind-read, and therefore may assume they're upset with us because of the short response.

We can also mind-read as a trauma response. Dr. Nicole LePera talks about this in her books and on her Instagram.[46] Your mind

---

[46] LePera, Nicole. *How to Do the Work: Recognize Your Patterns, Heal from Your Past, and Create Your Self.* Harper Wave, an Imprint of HarperCollinsPublishers, 2021.

reading may actually be a form of *emotional monitoring*. I know for me, this is a big part of why I mind-read. I would call my childhood household unconventional. My parents ran two businesses out of our house, so there were a lot of people around all of the time. Sometimes I'd come home and none of the people in my house were people who actually lived there. Being around that many personalities taught me at a young age to constantly monitor the mood.

As an adult, I've found one of the most important pieces of advice I've heard with regard to mind-reading is this: You're not responsible for what people don't tell you.

If someone is upset, it's their responsibility for them to tell you. And this goes for ourselves too! If we're upset enough to let it affect our interactions, we have the option to tell the people affected by our mood what is going on. But it isn't anyone else's responsibility to guess what's going on with us.

I really appreciate that my friends and I do this. It's as simple as sending a message that says, "Hey, I had a long day, so if my texts seem clipped, I'm not upset with you. I'm just drained." It's that easy.

And on the flip side, if you have someone who seems off, it's not your responsibility to put on your detective hat and solve the case of "What Did I Do To Offend Them." Chances are whatever's going on with them has nothing to do with you. And if it does have to do with you, it's their responsibility to come to you with the problem, not your responsibility to guess.

Try to stop mind-reading 1% more of the time, and to also be honest with your feelings (when appropriate). If someone seems upset with you, oh well! Unless they've expressed the problem, go on with your day. If you're upset with a person or situation, either talk it out with the person or consider letting people who may be affected by your mood know that it isn't about them.

As with most things, this is all easier said than done. But it's totally worth putting in the work.

Reflection

Mistakes

We all make them

Have you ever made a mistake? No, of course not. You're perfect. :)

But for those of us who have made mistakes, we've probably felt the shame that can come along with them. This is a huge bummer because mistakes are how we learn. There's a saying, "This isn't my first rodeo," but most of life is made up of "first rodeos." When you try something new, it's your first rodeo and you likely won't have a perfect performance. Even if it's your 100th rodeo, there's no guaranteeing perfection. And that's okay.

Believe it or not, there are lots of good reasons to make mistakes.[47] When you make a mistake, you have to think creatively about how not to make it again, which opens new neural pathways or reinforces lessons you've learned before. You also gain empathy for other people who make mistakes. Mistakes teach you to be brave, because admitting failure in any form can be intimidating. Mistakes also teach you a lot about yourself by how you react to them and how you treat yourself for making them.

If everything went perfectly all of the time, we wouldn't have products like penicillin, microwave ovens, bubble gum, and corn

---

[47] Lim, Crystie. "This Is Why You Should Be Proud of Making Mistakes." *LifeHack*, 25 Jan. 2021, www.lifehack.org/299971/this-why-you-should-proud-making-mistakes.

flakes. All of those were the products of someone making a mistake.

So the question is, how can you overcome the fear of making mistakes? The first step is to acknowledge the fear of making mistakes. When I was young, I was so shy that I later learned people thought I was stuck up. It was super hard for me to make friends because I never wanted to talk to anyone, afraid I would say something stupid and get made fun of. Over time, I forced myself to be social, to tell jokes, and join in the conversation. To this day, I remember some of the moments where I told a joke and it fell so flat that the silence was deafening.

But I kept practicing conversation even when I didn't know what to say. Fast forward to the present where I frequently have to present to groups of people. It's not unusual for me to find out what I'm presenting mere hours or even minutes before the meeting. In these contexts, it could be easy to get flustered and fear making a mistake, but I've recovered from all of my previous verbal blunders so I know I have the capacity to overcome any I might make while presenting. I've learned how to make friends with my mistakes, not berate myself over them.

Mistakes can be one of the greatest tools to help us grow, if we let them.

The idea of making a mistake can be scary, and the higher the stakes, the worse it can be. So why not create a space where it's okay for you to make mistakes? If you can't create that space for yourself in a high-pressure or public environment, do it at home.

Make dinner using a new recipe.

Draw a picture of a plant.

Do a puzzle without looking at the picture.

Learn a new language.

There are endless ways to give yourself the space to make potential mistakes and then learn from them.

The more you make mistakes and learn how to rebound, you start to build confidence in yourself and trust that you can handle whatever it is life is going to throw at you. This is how you start to break through the unrealistic idea of "perfectionism" in all aspects of your life.

Give yourself permission to make 1% more mistakes. Make the mistakes and learn from them, even if the learning is simply acknowledging that you survived the mistake. The more you practice this, the more you'll be able to learn from and trust yourself over time.

Reflection

Money

Get excited about money!

I saw a comic recently that said something to the effect of, "Going to work is so embarrassing. It's like broadcasting to everyone that you need money." I laughed because it's funny but it's also true! There can be so much shame around money that people may spend their entire lives battling their relationship with it. The book "Happy Money: The Japanese Art of Making Peace with Your Money" by Ken Honda[48] talks about this and a few of the lessons were so impactful that I want to share them.

The concept of the book is simple: money — like everything else — has an energy associated with it. But when it's *your* money, you are the one who decides what that energy is. Money that is happily spent has a good energy and that goodness will help it come back to you in time. Money that has bad energy will never want to return to you.

For example, when you pay your rent or mortgage, you can think, "There goes my hard earned cash into my landlord's/bank's pocket." OR you can think, "I'm so happy and thankful that I have this money to pay for a safe space to live." One clearly has more positive vibes than the other.

---

[48] Honda, Ken. *Happy Money: The Japanese Art of Making Peace with Your Money*. Gallery Books, 2019.

Another concept I thought was particularly interesting is to get excited when we receive money. Whether it was earned, given, won, etc., get excited like you would if it was a present someone gave you. It's GOOD to be happy and excited about money! You don't have to be ashamed or feel bad about it.

So how can you apply this and be 1% better today? Chances are that you have at least one expense today you would rather not deal with. Getting gas, buying eggs, paying your credit card. As you make that transaction, stop for a second and get happy. Conjure up the feeling of happiness that you are able to pay for that transaction. Even if paying that bill is a stretch right now, cultivating a grateful attitude around money will help it boomerang back to you. Since everything has energy, imbue that transaction with good energy, and you will become a magnet for good energy to return.

Reflection

Motivation

Finding motivation even when it's hard

We've all had those days when by the time we get home, there's zero motivation for anything. And if we don't have motivation, then we aren't going to be able to get the things done that we want to, even if it's something as simple as getting up to go do the dishes. But not to worry, there are lots of tips and tricks for how to get yourself motivated to go and do the things that matter to you.

Let's start with the five second rule, popularized by Mel Robinson. This is a great hack for when you truly can't get going no matter what. You simply count down from five and then like a rocket ship blasting off, you get up. She wrote an entire book on this method that digs into all of the science behind why this works, but for the sake of brevity, just know that it works and it's powerful. So the next time you want to get going but can't pull yourself out of bed or off the couch, just count down 5-4-3-2-1… blast off!

The other motivation method I want to mention is the five minute rule. I'm not sure if that's the official name but that's what I call it. Whatever task or activity it is you need to do, commit to doing it for five minutes. That's all. Just five minutes. If you find that you can keep going, do it for another five minutes, and so on. Some days, you might only do it for that first five minutes, and other days, you just keep on going. I use the five minute rule a lot for writing. I love writing. It is truly my passion in life. But very often if I get up early to write, I'm sleepy and can't get in a whole 45-60 minutes of writing, however I can certainly get in five minutes. The same is true about writing later in the day. If I can't sit down at my computer until 9 p.m. or 10 p.m. then I know I don't have a lot of creative juice left, but if I can get five minutes of writing in, sometimes I find that I have another five minutes after that, and another five minutes after that. I also find this method helpful when I want to go running or something similar. I commit to doing it for five minutes, and if it feels good, I keep going.

If you continue to encounter a task or activity that you truly, no matter what, can't find the motivation to get done, maybe that's a good, gentle nudge that it isn't right for you. Not everything in life should feel hard all of the time. At some point, you have to decide, even if you have a very good "why," does it feel aligned with the kind of life you want to have?

Can you try to find just 1% more motivation throughout your day? Even if you only start a task but don't complete it, give yourself a pat on the back because you tried and some days, trying is the best we can do. And that's okay!

Reflection

Movement

It's time to get moving

After I broke my ankle and was re-learning to walk, I kept making the joke that if you don't use your body, it deteriorates, but if you do use your body, it deteriorates. Which can be true if you treat your body at two different extremes, but somewhere in the middle is the normal movement that we are all capable of every day, and that's the sweet spot.

This isn't a chapter about fitness, so don't get jumpy. It's a chapter about general movement for overall wellbeing. Hear me out...

Movement is important for blood flow, stimulating our lymphatic system, removing toxins from your body — good stuff that keeps your little body machine humming along. But it's also good for keeping the flow of energy in your body going so that it doesn't get stuck. There are thousands of years of proof of this type of movement in the form of qigong, tai chi, and other energetic modalities. Think back to a time when you felt off or stuck and you went for a walk or did some other activity to get your body going. It was helpful, right?

Somatics is another modality that can help you move your energy around and start feeling good again. It's not a new science, but it is gaining popularity as people seek alternative treatments for things like anxiety, burnout, and trauma recovery. Once I learned about it,

I decided to give it a try and from the beginning, I was so hooked that I even got certified to teach it. When boiled down, it's basically the practice of moving. If I'm stressed, I go find somewhere to be alone and tense up my body then release it. I repeat this until the stress flows through and out of my body. If I'm anxious, I can jump around or shake and wiggle my body until it feels like all that pent-up energy has moved on. These are simple, but powerful ways to find instant relief to uncomfortable or stressful situations by moving your body in subtle ways.

One easy way to start incorporating movement into your life is when you feel a sensation or pain in your body, stop and stretch it out or make some other motion that alleviates it. Sometimes my right shoulder tenses up when I'm stressed, and I know that's my queue to get off the computer and go stretch and move around. Or at the very minimum, take a few deep breaths, visualizing the tension leaving my shoulder. Don't forget that breathing also counts as movement as well! When you take a breath deep into your diaphragm, you're engaging lots of muscles and organs as well as bringing fresh, clean oxygen into your body.

It's shockingly easy to make movement a consistent, healing part of our lives, we've just been overthinking it. The next time you're feeling energy getting stuck in your body, can you try moving it out rather than letting it settle in your system? If you're so inclined, maybe look up some qigong or tai chi classes near you (or online) to learn their timeless methods of using movement for overall balance and wellbeing. Movement is so important, but we need to go with the flow to make it work for us.

Reflection

Negativity

You are in control of the negativity in your life

Every day we encounter situations that are negative and have the potential to bring us down. But the good news is that you are in control of how much you let it affect you. Whether it's a situation at work, difficult friends and family, or a personal issue you're working on, you control how much you let it bother you. You also control what you let into your life.

Have you ever noticed that tasks feel much harder to accomplish when they're mired in negativity? If you have to wake up early to do something exciting, it's usually a lot easier to pop up when the alarm goes off than it is if you're dreading what lies ahead for you that day.

Does this mean you can never be negative ever? Absolutely not. Sometimes life straight up sucks. Loved ones die, people lose their jobs, lose their homes, get sick, the list goes on. And sometimes even minor inconveniences and frustrations can stack up and it feels like the world is on your shoulders. So, what do you do to get out from under that pile of negativity?

One tactic I was recently introduced to that I love is the idea of "emptying your cup." This is where you tell a friend, trusted confidant, a therapist, or even just write in a journal all the things that are weighing on you, emptying your emotional cup of all of the problems that have been dragging you down. By doing this, you aren't ruminating, but instead you're getting the thoughts out of your system so you can move on.

Be careful not to talk about the problems ad nauseam though, because that's just reinforcing them. I love the saying, "If talking about a problem over and over again solved it, don't you think it would have been fixed by now?"

Just empty your cup, freeing up mental and emotional space to move on from the issue that's causing negativity and find more positive aspects of your day to focus on. Maybe even take a moment to visualize an empty cup, and then visualize filling it up with a bright white light, or whatever other image conjures up a positive feeling for you.

Though it may not feel like it, at any given moment, we have the choice to find positivity or negativity. Of course, occasionally we are so down in the dumps because of depression, grief, or some other unavoidable feeling, that it feels impossible to pull ourselves out of it. In those moments, simply being gentle with yourself, validating your feelings, and understanding that it won't always feel this way, these are all ways of sprinkling in some positive healing for yourself.

Removing negativity can very often be done simply by not feeding more into it.

Can you identify areas of your life that you feel negatively towards and find a way to shine a more positive light on them? If you can't find a bright side on your own, ask a friend to help. You have options!

Reflection

Newness

You are new in each moment

Did you know that you can have a fresh start whenever you want one? If you screwed up five minutes ago, good news: that was an old version of you. This version right now learned from the screw up and is now a wiser version of yourself. You're a new person!

I am a person who takes care of my stuff. I was raised to believe that we are stewards of whatever we have, merely taking care of it for the moment. So, when I scratch or break something, I get this intense sense of guilt. I feel like I'm careless and unworthy of the item in the first place. But that is truly a terrible way to go through life because accidents happen. Life happens! No one can control everything.

Knowing that's how my brain works, it's not hard to imagine why this idea of being a new, fresh version of myself was freeing. The person who made those mistakes helped create the version of me that I am now, but I am different from that person. I am new.

One of my all time favorite tweets reflects this perfectly. It's a post from a person named Myrna Tellingheusen who is dubbed, "The internet's funniest grandma." In this viral tweet she wrote, "The outburst I had at JoAnn's Fabrics is not reflective of who I am."

We have all had moments that weren't our best. Moments when we failed, when we lost our temper, when we made the lazy decision. Those don't have to define who you are now. Right now, you are a person who overcame the circumstances that caused you to do the thing you wish you hadn't.

Life isn't static. It changes from day to day. This is why conventional wisdom says that whatever is most important for you to do, get it done in the morning. Because you never know what curveballs you might get during the day. You may even wind up face-to-face with an upset Myrna Tellingheusen in JoAnn's Fabrics, or worse, *being* like Myrna.

I am unintentionally awkward a lot of the time. It's just how I am. In the past, I was so embarrassed when I said or did something awkward and I'd ruminate about it all day. But one day, I decided that I was just going to own it. In that moment, the new Natalie was a person who could joke about the awkwardness instead of striving to cover it up (which always made every situation 1,000% more awkward anyway). Now, I'm just me! I don't worry that I'll say awkward things. In fact, I know there's a good chance that I will, and if that happens, I'll just own it and move on. But I wouldn't have the freedom to do that if I didn't allow myself to become new at each moment.

Logically, the argument against this is that *other people* know the version of you that screwed up. Other people saw your mistake, failure, or embarrassment. And that's tough because we all want to foster connections with people but in the end… so what? If anyone brings up your own personal Myrna Moment, remind yourself that was a past version of you. Be grateful for the lessons that version taught you and move on. In the end, what people think of you truly doesn't matter. Every single person who knows you holds a different version of you in their heads influenced by their own preconceived notions and your interactions. It is impossible to impact how someone sees you. So, let it go. All that matters is what you think of you. Cliché but true.

Guess what? You, the person reading this line, are different from the person who started reading this chapter. You have new information. You (hopefully) have laughed a little. You are thinking introspectively.

Give yourself permission to hit the "Reset" button whenever you want to. Reset and know that you are a new person who is wise enough now to know you need a reset. Instead of berating yourself for failures and bad decisions, understand you've gained valuable knowledge and continue on with this new, wiser you.

Reflection

Opinions

What do you think of yourself?

I would venture to guess that the majority of people reading this grew up in communities with some kind of social pressure to conduct themselves in a particular way. Because while social ties are pivotal to living long, healthy lives, they're also something that can make us confused about who we are as individuals.[49]

If you're always seeing yourself through the lens of other people, how will you ever know the most authentic version of yourself?

There's a video clip of Dieon Sanders, the head coach of the University of Colorado's football team, and former pro sports star. There's no love lost between Sanders and the press, so the way he responded to a particular question struck me:

"What about me would make you think that I would care about your opinion about me? Your opinion of me is not the opinion that I have of myself. You ain't make me, so you can't break me. You ain't build me, so you can't kill me. God established me. So there's ain't nothing you could do to me. I wish the world thought like that.

"Youngsters, do not give a darn what opinions people have of you. As long as that opinion is not consistent with that of yourself,

---

[49] "An Active Social Life May Help You Live Longer." *Harvard T.H. Chan School of Public Health*, 22 Nov. 2024, hsph.harvard.edu/news/active-social-life-longevity/.

you be you. I'm not planning to make you feel good about me. I already feel good about me. I'm good."

In a world where everyone wants to be an influencer, get likes, go viral, be relevant... we've got to first look inward to our opinions of ourselves. Who are you? Are you living your life in a way that reflects yourself?

This is really hard. I don't want to make it sound easy. It's much more comfortable to follow the crowd and do things you know are acceptable. And if you expose an authentic, vulnerable side of yourself and people don't like it, that hurts way more than if people don't like a version of yourself you were just putting out there to be part of the group.

Authenticity and vulnerability go hand in hand.

The summer before my sophomore year of college, I worked a full time corporate job during the day, and part time at a gym in the evenings. Towards the end of summer, I'd worked myself to the point of being sick. I put my two weeks in at the gym, and found out the owner had been saying some very unkind things about me when I wasn't around. She was friends with my parents so I asked to speak with her. She was shocked to learn I'd heard what she said about me (though she didn't deny it), and I let her know the main reason I was there was to ensure that me ending my tenure there a few weeks early wouldn't reflect badly on my parents.

While that may have been a "mature" choice at the time, looking back I'm like... why the heck did I care what she thought of me? A full grown adult woman was spending her time gossiping about a

19yo who worked 15 hour days. Her opinion of me meant so much at the time that I felt like I needed to make it right.

There is a scientific explanation for this and it's pretty simple: we want people to like us.[50] Being liked often gives us power, money, status, and other things people strive for. It matters because you're embedded in a community by being liked.

But it's not healthy to care about what anyone thinks about you except for yourself.

We're human though, so when the need arises to be liked even at the expense of being yourself, remember there are people all over the globe who have similar interests, sense of humor, sense of values, etc. You may not have found them yet, but that shouldn't stop you from exploring and expressing who you are.

So when others voice an opinion about you, it may make you feel some type of way. But if you tap into that higher opinion you have of yourself, the rest fades away. And sure, maybe most of us have poor opinions of ourselves and that's why we look elsewhere. Spend time working on that.

Remember:

You are here for a reason.

There are no accidents.

You are made of the same building blocks as the planets, stars, and galaxies.

---

[50] "What Does It Mean to Be Human?: Social Life." *The Smithsonian Institution's Human Origins Program*, 3 Jan. 2024, humanorigins.si.edu/human-characteristics/social-life.

You are the only one of you who will ever exist.

And if all of that doesn't make you realize how special you are — no matter what anyone else thinks — here's a slightly morbid thought that I've found helpful in the past. How many people can you vividly remember from three generations ago? Maybe a handful? When we die, so does what other people think of us. A select few stories may live on, but it's all forgotten in the end.

So be yourself! Life is too short to be anyone else.

Try to be 1% better by putting your opinion of yourself first. Post that meme that maybe only you think is funny. Start that project you've been putting off because someone made you second guess whether you could do it or not. Challenge negative thoughts you have about yourself because you are awesome!

Reflection

Patience

Patience is transformative

If you're anything like me, you saw the title of this post and thought, "I don't want to read that," or maybe even, "I don't have time to read that." If you had a similar reaction, this post is for you.

We've all heard that "patience is a virtue" but it's also really, really good for you. Here are some benefits[51]:

Patience increases your mental health by helping you feel more satisfied with your life.

Patience in the face of boring, monotonous situations helps you feel more hopeful and less frustrated.

Patience makes us more "agreeable" which in turn makes us better friends and neighbors.

Patience helps us reach our goals.

Patience increases our physical health by decreasing the chance of illnesses like "headaches, acne flare-ups, ulcers, diarrhea, and pneumonia."

You probably already guessed patience helps with many of these things, but I was still pleasantly surprised to see there were so many scientific studies to back it up.

So, where do we even begin when we want to start being more patient?

---

[51] Newman, Kira. "Four Reasons to Cultivate Patience." *Greater Good*, greatergood.berkeley.edu/article/item/four_reasons_to_cultivate_patience.

The first step is to be more aware of when you're being reactionary to situations and try to let go of the frustration building up inside you.

For example, someone is telling you a long story and you've tried several verbal cues to tell them to wrap it up (like saying "That's crazy" at least 5x, probably more). When you notice yourself getting impatient, take a deep breath and exhale to release the frustration. Recognize that this person is sharing something in an effort to connect with you, and that's pretty cool.

Or maybe you're stuck in traffic, behind a slow walker, or in a line that just won't move. Again, take a deep breath, exhale the frustration and accept that being impatient isn't going to make this situation move any faster. Acknowledge instead of react.

You can also practice being patient with yourself, then apply those same principles to dealing with other people and life situations.

I often think about one instance where I saw my sister exhibit incredible patience. My niece was crying in her highchair and we couldn't figure out what she wanted. Instead of getting frustrated, my sister took a deep breath, smiled at her daughter and said, "I love you so much." And just like that, my niece calmed down.

What if we treated ourselves and others like that when we get impatient? How much more inner peace and health benefits could we reap simply by acknowledging the situation rather than reacting?

The good (and maybe bad) news is that we have LOTS of opportunities to practice patience throughout the day. So the next time you feel the wave of impatience building, stop yourself, take a deep breath, and let it go before doing or saying anything from a place of impatience. Each time you do that, you'll make yourself a little bit better.

What are some other ways that help you exhibit patience?

Reflection

Perfection

Perfection stunts progress

I am a recovering perfectionist. I never thought of myself as a perfectionist because I never really cared what grades I got in school as long as I got a B or higher. But once I started working on projects for myself, things that I loved and cared about, I became a bit fanatical about making sure everything was perfect. Since I put so much effort into it, any critique felt like a personal slight and I'd get really defensive about it. Until one of my friends said he was getting a tattoo that said "Progress, not perfection." At first, I thought that was the dumbest thing ever because who wouldn't just want perfection? But as I've gotten older and gained the perspective of life experience, I now feel that phrase deep within my core.

Perfection steals progress away from us. If we are too scared to put our work into the world until it's perfect, then we are holding back from sharing our gifts with others. Whenever I'm talking to other writers who want to publish their own book but are scared it isn't good enough, I ask them is it the best it can be right now? Because if the answer is yes, then that is more than enough. If we are living our life in a healthy way, then we are always going to learn more and become better than we are today. I always say that while I try my best with every book, painting, embroidery, whatever it is, the second it's over, I've already become a smarter, more talented person than I was when I started because that project contributed to my growth. Does that mean I abandon what I've done and start over? Absolutely not. Your work deserves to be seen and recognized! And you are so brave for putting yourself out there knowing that though you want things to be as perfect as they can, you are not letting perfectionism hold you back.

If you want to start overcoming perfectionism, start by simply being kind to yourself. There are studies showing perfectionism can be a learned behavior but it can also be genetic. So acknowledge that there's nothing wrong with you, and you're functioning perfectly according to the lot you were given in life. Then, acknowledge that nothing will be perfect, so just do it anyway. Perfectionism causes us to freeze in our lives and robs us of the ability to chase our dreams. When you kindly give yourself permission to do something, knowing that you are making progress towards your goals, you start to heal from perfectionism.

If possible, try embracing imperfection. Remember that you are human and not being perfect is part of the human experience. If everything was perfect all of the time, it would lose the beautiful unpredictability of life. Imperfection makes things interesting. I recently heard someone talking about art and they said, "If I wanted it to look exactly like the real thing, I'd go buy a photograph. I want to know how the artist sees it and interprets it." That means creating an "imperfect" yet beautiful representation of whatever they are creating, and that makes the art perfect in its own wonderful way.

You can do that too! Think of a part of your life where perfectionism is holding you back. Can you put a little bit more of yourself into it and show it to the world, even if it means facing your greatest fears of imperfection? Can you put your focus into the process of what you're doing instead of the end product? When we let ourselves get caught up in the moment, in the flow of creation, then that's what's really important. If you can do that and put your whole self into it, then it's already "perfect."

Reflection

Perspective

Embrace your own perspective

Have you ever met someone and no matter what, you couldn't see eye-to-eye on something? That's because you were both coming at something from different perspectives. Different perspectives make the world go 'round. It's how we're able to have new thoughts and ideas by seeing something in a different light. And sometimes our perspectives don't align with other people's, but we can still benefit from an exchange of thoughts.

When I was thinking about how to illustrate this, I thought of the show *Survivor*. It's going on its 50th season and in that time, viewers have gotten to see how each player approaches the game differently. Some absolutely refuse to tell a lie and it costs them the game while it may make others winners. Some tell lie after lie and they come out on top. Even within the same season, you'll hear one person say they played with integrity while another rips them for being a backstabber. They both have a different perspective of what integrity means. But it's not only that. At the end of the season, the remaining players need to make a case to a jury of people they've voted out of the game as to why they deserve to win the $1 million. Each jury member votes based on *their own* perspective of what makes someone a sole survivor. That may be performing well in challenges, while in many cases the winner is someone who rode the coattails of a more aggressive player, saving them from doing any interpersonal dirty work. You never know from season to season what strategy will win out because it all depends on the perspective of the players and the people sitting on the jury.

Perspectives are squishy and can change throughout our lives, but at any given moment, we are experiencing our world through our perspective right then. But that also means that you can change your perspective if you don't like how the current view makes you feel. Sometimes that can mean trying to put yourself in someone else's shoes in order to see the situation from their perspective. Maybe you'll gain new insight as to why they're handling a certain situation the way they are and it will make it easier for you to get along with them.

When I start to feel upset or tense when I ruminate about a situation, I try to stop myself and challenge the thought that triggered the feeling. I ask myself, what is making me feel like this? Can I reframe it from a different perspective? If not, why? Sometimes the answer is as simple as, I don't want to change my perspective because I'm nervous that will mean that I'm wrong and other people will see that I'm wrong. But here's the thing… it is almost certain that everyone already knows I'm wrong and I'm just the last to admit it to myself! That change in perspective can have a big effect on relationships.

Some other powerful tools to help you see things from a different perspective are to literally seek out different perspectives that may challenge your own. Talk to someone who you know feels differently on a topic than you do. You don't have to agree with them, but it may help you understand where they're coming from, and in having the conversation you may help them gain perspective too.

A quick way to change your perspective is to do something that makes you feel good and puts you in a positive frame of mind. Go for a walk. Take a nap. Phone a friend. Whatever it is, changing into a positive mindstate can help change your perspective.

Just remember that we all have different perspectives, so accept that maybe you will never be able to see the world exactly as someone else does. BUT you *can* try to shift your own perspective to one that feels good and authentic to you. You can't control other people's perspective, but you can always control your own.

Your entire life is played out through your own perspective. Can you try to make it feel just 1% better for yourself? Whether that's exploring your own feelings or broadening your view of the world, your perspective is what you make of it.

Reflection

Presence

Be here now

There's a Tennessee Williams quote that I think about often. It goes:

"Life is all memory, except for the present moment that goes by you so quick you hardly catch it going."

I love that it puts an urgency on being in the present moment. We're often so busy that we become impatient for the current moment to pass by so we can get to the next thing, and then the present moment misses us completely.

Studies done on mindfulness suggest that when people are grounded in the present moment, they show improved mental health and overall higher levels of happiness.[52,53] This is even true when the present moment is a painful one. Living *through* the moment instead of pushing away the discomfort results in less pain than it otherwise would.

Think about the last time you had a task you felt anxious about so you kept putting it off. When you finally did it, the task likely

---

[52] Halliwell, Ed. "The Science and Practice of Staying Present through Difficult Times." *Mindful*, 16 Dec. 2024, www.mindful.org/science-practice-staying-present-difficult-times/.

[53] Kiken, Laura G, et al. "Being Present and Enjoying It: Dispositional Mindfulness and Savoring the Moment Are Distinct, Interactive Predictors of Positive Emotions and Psychological Health." *Mindfulness*, U.S. National Library of Medicine, Oct. 2017, www.ncbi.nlm.nih.gov/pmc/articles/PMC5755604/.

wasn't as hard as you'd built it up to be and you feel a great relief that it's done with.

Our brains want to protect us from pain, so it makes sense that it would blow new or uncomfortable situations out of proportion. The brain likes what it knows. But what's comfortable often isn't what will make us happy, it won't help us grow into the people we want to be.

Take this current moment, for example. You are reading this and you don't know what I'm going to write next. That might make your brain tell you to stop reading because what if you read something you don't want to know? Maybe it's trying to distract you with other thoughts so you don't keep reading. Imagine how much harder it would try to do that if I'd started this post with something ominous?

Being present gives us wholly new opportunities to experience our world. No two days are ever the same no matter how similar they may be.

So, what are some techniques for being more present in life?

Be aware of your thoughts. If this isn't a normal thing for you to do, set alarms at various times of the day and check in with yourself when they go off. What were you doing at that moment? What were you thinking about? If you want to take it a step further, write it down in a little notebook. Over time, you won't need the alarms and will naturally start checking in with yourself throughout the day.

Set intentions for the day. In reiki, we have five principles we reaffirm daily:

Just for today, I will not be angry.

Just for today, I will not worry.

Just for today, I will be grateful.

Just for today, I will do all my life's work honestly.

Just for today, I will be kind to all living things.

Consider using these phrases or making your own that you'll say to start the day. It doesn't mean that you won't mess up, but it does mean that you will try your best to abide by them. In doing this, your actions become moments of self-reflection in the present.

Do one activity mindfully. This means making an effort to pay attention to every moment while doing the activity. You can do this while eating, going on a walk, taking a shower, cooking, etc. While you do the activity, take in what all of your five senses are experiencing at that moment.

As always, we are all different individuals, so what helps one person find presence may not work for the next. Experiment with various tactics throughout your day and see which one works best for you.

If you can, try to notice 1% more of what's happening right now in this moment before it becomes another memory. What would life look like if we made it a point to experience it as it happens?

Reflection

Pride

You deserve to be proud of yourself!

There's an old saying that "pride comes before a fall" but I worry that over time we've all taken that phrase a bit too far. For some of us, exhibiting a sense of pride may feel a little unusual if not downright uncomfortable. That makes it hard when we want to celebrate our own wins because that's seen as "bad."

But if you break down the word "pride" and the different ways it can be used, the layers of the word begin to show themselves.

Being prideful is "having an excessively high opinion of oneself."

Being proud is "feeling deep pleasure or satisfaction as a result of one's own achievements, qualities, or possessions, or those of someone with whom one is closely associated."

However, it's a slippery slope from being proud to being prideful. The secondary definition of proud is "having or showing a high or excessively high opinion of oneself or one's importance."

And there lies the delicate syntactical balance of being proud of yourself.

Feeling proud of yourself is actually deeply important with regard to your self-esteem and self-image.[54] We all do things that *should* make us feel proud of ourselves. But learning how to self-

---

[54] Kristenson, Sarah. "11 Steps to Feel More Proud of Yourself." *Happier Human*, 10 Apr. 2023, www.happierhuman.com/proud-yourself/.

congratulate — especially if you were taught from a young age that pride will lead to a downfall — can be particularly fraught.

A good barometer is motivation: are you exhibiting pride because you are genuinely proud of yourself or because you want to "brag" about your achievements?

Sometimes when we don't share the ways we are proud of ourselves, we rob the people we love of being able to share these exciting moments with us. So being proud of yourself, ironically, isn't always about you. Being vulnerable enough to tell people you're feeling proud helps build deeper connections and empathy with those around you. It also helps other people who may be averse to feeling self-pride.

Can you find 1% more opportunities to show that you are proud of yourself? It could be as simple as telling yourself in the mirror. If you feel so inclined, tell a friend something that you're proud of yourself for doing. There are parts of each day when even when we're feeling down, we can find ways to build ourselves up.

Reflection

Problems

Our brains are making stuff up

How many times have you been doing something (or doing nothing) then all of a sudden you get a creeping sensation in your mind. It makes you think… Something's not right here. You can't put your finger on it, but there's something wrong. Maybe you forgot to lock the door or turn off the oven. Maybe your friends are upset because you couldn't hang out this weekend. Maybe everyone you know is mad at you and that's why no one is returning your texts at this very second.

Sound familiar? The good news is that there's nothing wrong with you, there's probably nothing wrong at all, and you're not alone in feeling that something is amiss.

Our brain is a computer that is always on, which means it's creating problems for itself to solve. Think about your own computer, how it makes noises and keeps working even when you're not doing anything on it. That's how your brain is. To keep you alive (or "on") there are processes that need to happen continuously. So, in fact it is always solving problems all of the time.

The brain is wired to keep us alive, to scan for threats and help us defend ourselves against them. Unfortunately, in doing this, it sometimes makes us think there's a threat when there isn't.

I'll go back to the texting example because it's a common experience that comes up for people. We're hardwired for community and social connection. It's part of how we thrive as humans. So if you text someone and are expecting a text back immediately but don't get it, you may feel that your place within your social structure is compromised. This is a threat to your wellbeing, your happiness. Then it's up to you if you want to cycle down that thought spiral or remind yourself that people are busy. They have jobs, they might be driving, they might be sleeping. You don't know what's going on, but you do know that without more information, nothing has changed.

It reminds me of this Alice in Wonderland meme where Alice is talking with the Cheshire cat. The cat says the famous line, "We're all mad here." And Alice responded with, "At me?"

Another problem with problems is that our supercomputer brain likes to add to the equation, not subtract.[55] We wonder what else we can do to fix something rather than consider that taking away is an option as well. I'm very guilty of this. I'll say something and then try to talk my way out of it, digging a hole deeper and deeper until my friends kindly say, "Natalie, please, just stop talking." Reader, let me tell you that saying less has been an absolute game changer for me. Subtracting the words I thought I needed in order to solve a problem completely of my own making has been revelatory.

---

[55] Kwon, Diana. "Our Brain Typically Overlooks This Brilliant Problem-Solving Strategy." *Scientific American*, Scientific American, 20 Feb. 2024, www.scientificamerican.com/article/our-brain-typically-overlooks-this-brilliant-problem-solving-strategy/.

This is why people get worked up about the future. We don't know what's going to happen, but our brain wants to prepare us for every possible scenario — often to our detriment! We think if we do more that we'll be more prepared for whatever lies ahead. But outside of making emergency kits and having an emergency plan, how can we really know what to prepare for? Chances are, we can't know. So we're doing more to solve an unknown problem, wasting our precious time and energy in the process.

If you struggle to sleep at night, you're not alone and this problem-solving function of your brain may be largely to blame. When we put our heads on our pillows, it's probably the first time all day that you've slowed down. Well, doesn't that sound like a perfect time for your brain to unleash all of the future problems it's been storing up all day for you to think about later?

Will your child get into the right school? Do you even know what the right school is? Did you remember to put gas in the car or do you have to stop before work? Is climate change going to wash away or burn up your home? Do you even like this home that much? Will interest rates drop low enough for you to get a new home before you outgrow this one? What about your emergency supplies — are they expired? Are you really happy or are you faking it? Did you remember to lock the back door? … You get the idea. Endless, endless worries all tallied up by your brain to try and keep you alive, while slowly driving you insane.

Okay, so what do you do to stop it? Meditation is a good practice to start, but I know a lot of people don't like full-on meditation. If you don't want to give it a try, don't worry. Simply take a deep breath (inhale through your nose and exhale through your mouth) to calm down your nervous system and remind yourself that in this moment, right now, nothing is wrong. These concerns rattling around in your mind will be addressed in time, but you don't need to right now. One by one, let the worries go.

Here's what I like to do: I spend a second or two acknowledging each new problem that pops into my head, I thank my brain for trying to keep me safe, and then I let it go. I don't engage with the thought any further.

And when that doesn't work, I ask myself, "Am I doing or can I do anything about this right now?" The answer is almost always no. So, I let it go. It's illogical to ruminate on something that I am unwilling or unable to do anything about. I've actually found that, for me, this is the most powerful way to stop a worry cycle.

The next time you notice problems start making their way into your thoughts, try to let 1% of them go. Thank your brain for trying to keep you alive and safe, and then move on. Find a method that works for you when you start falling into a spiral. If you can't or won't do anything about the problem right then, let it go.

Reflection

Purpose

What is your purpose?

When I was in high school I read Rick Warren's book "The Purpose Driven Life," and it left me feeling more confused and empty than before I'd started it. I did the workbook, I re-read it, and I was still left feeling like I had even less of a sense of purpose than before I'd read it. I've spent a lot of my life thinking about my purpose and what it might be, and until a couple of years ago, I only came up with vague ideas.

So what changed? How did I figure out my purpose?

One day, it hit me out of nowhere. I always thought my purpose had to be some big, world-changing thing. After all, my purpose is the very reason for my existence, the reason I am alive, surely it needed to require time, effort, sacrifice. It had to be something that left behind deep footprints and marked change in people's lives.

But then I realized there is equal purpose found in the small things. I realized my purpose is writing, storytelling, and creating art. At first, I had to convince myself that storytelling could even be a life's purpose, that it was something worth dedicating my life to. How can telling stories possibly be a person's life purpose?

Well, bards and traveling storytellers are the reasons we have a lot of the legends we have today. People watch TV and movies to escape or relax, and those require storytelling. Even creating a work of non-fiction necessitates an element of storytelling. By being a storyteller, I'm helping people learn about themselves, maybe fire up their imaginations, take a moment to chill out, and probably more things I'm not aware of.

So, how do you find your purpose?

Well, that's kind of an individual experience. I've mentioned the book "Ikigai" before, and what Ikigai means is purpose. There are four questions to consider:

What do I love?

What am I good at?

What can I be paid for?

What does the world need?

This construct has been helpful for millions of people, and was actually recommended to me at work when I was contemplating a career change. If this four-part framework works for you, that's great! Use it!

Unfortunately for me, it brought me back to how I felt in high school. I don't think you need to be *good at* what your purpose is. After all, who decides what is good and what isn't? I also don't think being paid for what your purpose is a requirement. It's very possible to have a day job and still make time for other passions that impact people in a positive way. If the two intersect, that's great, but they may not and that doesn't preclude it from being your purpose. I think asking what the world needs is intimidating and off-putting. Thinking about how to impact *the world* makes it daunting to narrow down what your purpose might be.

No matter how you find your purpose, one thing is true: a sense of purpose is essential to mental and physical health and helps us create and maintain social ties.[56]

Now, it's time to ask yourself, what is your purpose? If you don't know, start by identifying what you love to do. Don't know what you love to do? As a workaholic, I've been there, too. I had to sit down, close my eyes, and think back to when I was a child. What did Little Natalie do when she was playing? She made up stories, put on puppet shows, crafted things with her hands. It turns out nothing has changed and those are still the activities I love, that I get lost in. Try tapping into your memory of what you did as a child that made you light up.

Start there, and think about how to integrate the activity into your daily adult life. Did you like playing games? Then try inventing some games of your own. Maybe you wanted to spend all of your time socializing and playing with friends. Then get involved with some local programs within your communities or organize a charity event. Did you like reading books? Start doing book reviews on your own blog or sites like Goodreads. You never know where life will take you once you start believing in yourself.

You matter, and you have a purpose. You are on Earth during this exact time period for a reason. Dig into your purpose 1% more; get 1% better at tapping into it and integrating it into your daily life.

---

[56] Hill, Patrick L, and Nicholas A Turiano. "Purpose in Life as a Predictor of Mortality across Adulthood." *Psychological Science*, U.S. National Library of Medicine, July 2014, pmc.ncbi.nlm.nih.gov/articles/PMC4224996/.

The more you intentionally practice living your purpose every day, the more alive you'll feel. And when you do it, do it with (you guessed it) purpose.

Reflection

Reality

Non-woowoo ways to shape your experience

Believe it or not, you can create your reality, or at least the part of it that you're in control of. While we can't always influence or predict events like car accidents, layoffs, or global events, what we can do is create our own reality around them.

For example, you've likely heard the phrase "glass half empty or half full." An individual's response to that is them creating their reality. If the glass is half full, that means the viewpoint is there's such an abundance of water that even though the person drank some, there's still half of it left for them later. However, if the glass is half empty, there's now a viewpoint of water scarcity and it must be preserved.

Our reality is the same way. Jennice Vilhauer Ph.D. offers the idea of going to a party where 10 people complimented your outfit but one person said it was "interesting."[57] If you already have a poor self image, you're likely to fixate on the person who said it was "interesting" because that validates and reinforces your current self image. However, if you have a good self image, you may forget or not even care about the ambiguous comment, or even the

---

[57] Vilhauer Ph.D., Jennice. "How Your Thinking Creates Your Reality." *Psychology Today*, Sussex Publishers, www.psychologytoday.com/us/blog/living-forward/202009/how-your-thinking-creates-your-reality.

positive ones, because you know you felt confident about yourself and your outfit.

The placebo effect is another example of us creating our own reality. When testing new drugs, sometimes there is one group who receives a placebo pill, or a pill that does nothing. But the patients won't know which they're receiving. In many cases, even those who took the drugless placebo pills still experience measured improvement in their illness. When we are told something and believe it, our brain helps us validate that reality. If we think we are getting better and healing, then it will work with you to help you recover.

This isn't to say that you should push down and ignore emotions or feel responsible when bad things happen to you. Sometimes, that's just life. But you *are* able to control how you respond to life. Feel your emotions, and then find a way to move forward using the outlook you want to reflect in your reality. If you are struggling in a class or to learn a concept, instead of beating yourself up about it, start telling yourself you're great at it.

One of my mentors once told me that she's not sure if she's innately good at math or not, but she grew up with her parents telling her that she was, so she believed it. I, a person who was told by my teachers that I wasn't good at math, have spent my whole life believing that I'll "never learn." So, when I had to pass math-based classes in my MBA program, I'd reflexively have anxiety before anything was even assigned. But over time, I'd approach each test with the attitude that I was good at math and this was going to be a cinch. Logically, my past record with math didn't reflect this reality, but I didn't care. I was tired of being "bad at math" and believing the reinforcement of those perceived weaknesses. So, I just made myself believe I was good at math. Shockingly but maybe not all that surprising considering I was hyping myself up, I got an A+ in my statistics class and Bs in the other math-based classes.

So, the way that we participate in creating our reality is (1) by acknowledging that we can only control ourselves and our reactions to people and events. We have to release wanting to control other aspects; and (2) by empowering ourselves to be who we want to be and how we want our lives to feel.

How can you influence your reality 1% more? Can you tell yourself you're good at something even if you maybe don't believe it yet? Can you affirm your choices in a way that makes you immune to the comments of others? Can you shift your outlook on a situation so that it can bring you joy or at the very least not bring you pain? Take the time to be aware of your thoughts when you have them and identify patterns that you can tweak to start influencing your reality in a positive way.

Reflection

Relax

It may take a little effort

I have a confession to make: learning to relax is something that I've been working on for years. As much as I love lounging around and doing nothing all day, I also love having lots of projects and creative endeavors going at the same time. So this often means that when I give my brain the break it needs, I just sit there thinking about all of the fun, creative things I could be doing instead. And then there's the never-ending "to do" list of things I should actually be doing. There's so much going on that it feels like I'm wasting time if I chill out and relax.

There will always be something to do; something that must be done; something you want to do. But *doing* isn't always the best course of action. Then how can a person relax when there's so much going on and when, in some cases, people might actually not know how to relax?

The first point to remember is that relaxation looks different for each of us. To find your own personal relaxation style, think about what you'd do if you were on vacation with no obligations, responsibilities, or budget concerns. Would you choose to engage in more active activities or would you rather chill and relax? Try to get as specific as possible in your mind about exactly what you'd do if you were on a relaxing getaway.

Surveys have been conducted over the years to try and find the answer to how long it takes to fully decompress and unplug from work when you're on vacation. The answer varies somewhere between several days to around two weeks. For many people, that's longer than the vacation is itself. So, it's no wonder we've all forgotten how to really relax.

One of my favorite stories about the importance of relaxing and unplugging is that of Ian Fleming, the author of the James Bond novels. He would take two months off every year (typically in the winter) to fly to his Jamaican home, which he named Goldeneye. During this time, he'd swim in the morning, write during the day, and then go into town to socialize in the evening. He found a way to do all of the things that brought him joy, fired up his brain, and also helped him relax. While that's a great example of how relaxation can fuel our passions, it can also be a little demoralizing to those of us who don't have a tropical vacation home and can't leave our life behind for two months every year. So, what can we do to distill that feeling and make it come alive in our own lives?

When we try to squeeze that magic combo into our regular, everyday lives it's no surprise that it's initially difficult to find deep relaxation. What can be done to find this internal zen space where your body and mind can unwind and let go, where your nervous system can reset?

Let's think back to what activities you would do if you were on vacation right now. Now think if there's a way to find slivers of that in your day. If you like to explore on vacation, then explore around where you live. Eat at a different restaurant that you've wanted to try, or go sit at the park on a sunny day and take in the surroundings. If you like to lounge, give yourself permission to sit and do nothing for as long as you're able. I find that saying outloud to myself, "I am allowed to lie down and rest," is almost instantly calming. Play around with different techniques and find the ones that give you whatever sense of relaxation you're looking for.

Remember: you never need to feel guilty about relaxing. Allowing rest into our lives creates space for more of what we want to welcome into it.

It may seem counterintuitive, but schedule in 1% more time to experiment with different ways to relax. Once you become more familiar with how to chill out, then it'll become a natural part of your life. But for those of us who think there's no time to relax, then it's especially important for you to work relaxing into your schedule so you can prove to your brain that it is possible for you to incorporate these behaviors into your life.

Reflection

Rejection

Rejections are guideposts

Do you ever wish there was a little voice who could tell you what to do in life so you didn't have to figure it out on your own? The good news is, there is! The bad news is that we often see it as a negative thing instead of a helpful guide. It's rejection.

Of course, rejection shouldn't be minimized, and with good reason. Studies show that the body releases the same chemicals when you are rejected as when you are in physical pain. The body wants to be soothed because the brain has interpreted that you are in pain. And this is in large part because we are social creatures. So when we experience rejection, we may interpret it as being rejected by society in one way or another.

If you are rejected from the job you want, you may interpret that as you not being good enough. If you're rejected from a competition, you may feel like you'll never be successful. Same for rejections from love interests, friends, other pieces of the social webs we weave. In addition to physical pain, you may feel emotional pain like jealousy, anger, loneliness, and shame.

So, with all of that at stake, why would anyone ever want to put themselves out there for anything?

Because you get immediate feedback on the path that's meant for you!

I was so sure I wanted to be a sports journalist. I went to school for it, I wrote for some well-known publications, and I created a decently large network of other sportscasters. But no matter how hard I tried, how much free work I did, how many extra assignments I picked up, it just never happened for me.

I don't know what my life would have looked like if I'd become a professional sports reporter. I now see folks who started at the same publications at the same time as me and they're on TV living the dream. But what I realized over time is they live to work, not work to live. Now that I have the life I do, I can confidently say I'm grateful for the rejections because I love the life I built thanks to the guidance from hundreds of rejections.

Enough about me, let's talk about you. Take a minute and think about your latest rejection. Give yourself space to acknowledge and accept how it felt. Now take a moment and think about how it may have been pushing you towards or away from something else.

Would that friend group that you got squeezed out of have helped your overall wellbeing and path in life? Would that relationship you really wanted to work out have guided you towards a life abundant with opportunities for self-growth? Would that job you interviewed for have offered you the work-life balance you need at this time in your life? Would winning that competition have added to your life or taken away time from other important parts like time with your friends and family?

Coming to terms with rejection also helps us more gently reject other people and situations. We get the opportunity to be their gentle guidepost. When something isn't working — a project, a creative partnership, a friendship — you can find a way to be more gentle and constructive. In rejection, we can express and accept kindness. We can find gratitude for the person or situation that rejected us so we could find firmer footing on the path that's meant for us. And when we reject someone, we can choose to do it with kindness to gently nudge them towards their best path.

It makes me think of a fender bender I got into. A young driver sideswiped me, so we pulled over and exchanged information and were on our way. My immediate thought was: this accident was for him to learn something by getting into an accident with a chill, nice person instead of some road rager. The accident was something he needed on his driving journey, and I was chosen to be a guidepost.

That's how I think of rejection. Everyone is playing their parts nudging each other along to find our best, highest paths.

BUT — and this is a big one — you can't participate if you don't try.

As hard and scary as it is, put yourself out there for something. Whether you want to join a new social group, or you want to submit something to a contest, give it a try! And try it with the intention of testing the waters, seeking out a guidepost. When you ask the universe for feedback, you will get it.

Do you struggle with rejection because you feel that physical and social pain when you receive it? Can you find one thing to do this week that will gently test your limits of rejection with the intention to help you along on your path? Can you apply for the job you think is out of your wheelhouse but interests you? Can you go on a date? Can you join a local pick-up game for a sport you love? Can you share your opinion about something you love on a platform where you feel comfortable doing so?

If you learn to reframe rejection into a constructive tool that will guide you to the life you want (even if you don't think or know it right now), then it becomes a sigh of relief.

Reflection

Resilience

You've got this

I love the phrase, "Remember that you've already survived 100% of your hardest days." But how? How did I make it through the times that felt so hard I thought I'd crumble? The answer is resilience.

I got curious about this and wanted to learn more about why we need to be resilient in order to grow. Why can't life just be easy?

Well, it turns out that for the people who make life seem easy, they may just have a more positive take on negative situations. Studies show that children who grow up in similar or identical adverse environments can still have mentally positive outcomes depending on whether or not they have "at least one stable and committed relationship with a parent, caregiver, or other adult."[58] This person can help guide them during the tough moments. From there, as children grow up, they learn more coping skills that can help with resilience.

Some of these include:[59]

---

[58] "Inbrief: The Science of Resilience." *Center on the Developing Child at Harvard University*, 13 Dec. 2024, developingchild.harvard.edu/resources/inbriefs/inbrief-the-science-of-resilience/.
[59] Newman, Kira. "Five Science-Backed Strategies to Build Resilience." *Greater Good*, greatergood.berkeley.edu/article/item/five_science_backed_strategies_to_build_resilience.

- Expressive writing (writing for 20 minutes non-stop about the issue at hand, getting out all of your feelings and thoughts on the topic)
- Facing a fear
- Expressing self-compassion
- Meditating using MBSR (Palouse MBSR has a great course if you're interested)
- Forgiving others and yourself if needed
- Keeping your mind active to regularly practice problem solving

If you're still feeling less than resilient after reading these tips, give yourself some grace because there are other factors at play. It turns out that "33% to 53% [of] resilience appears to be passed down the generations."[60] Some people really are getting a head start when it comes to this trait.

Why is resilience important to cultivate? I'll spare you the neuroscience but it affects your stress response, your outlook on life, and your overall wellbeing. If you're more resilient, stressful situations become less stressful because you are able to handle them with more efficiency. When something happens, you can choose to look at it "glass half full" or "glass half empty." Both are true, but one will make you more optimistic and one will make you more pessimistic. This all contributes to your wellbeing because of the

---

[60] Parmar, MD., Rashmi. "The Science of Resilience and Wisdom." *Center for Practical Wisdom | The University of Chicago*, 10 May 2022, wisdomcenter.uchicago.edu/news/wisdom-news/science-resilience-and-wisdom

chemicals and neurotransmitters our brain and body release depending on how we've viewed the situation.

In other words, if you view a moment as taxing, exhausting, or negative, then you'll get a dose of cortisol released and your body will shift into a "fight, flight, or freeze" response. If you view it as a potential positive or neutral, you'll get a dose of "feel good" chemicals like dopamine.

We all have times in our lives where we need to persevere and be resilient in order to get through a tough moment. Think back to those times and recall the skills you used. And more importantly, give yourself credit for making it through the experience. Resilience comes in all shapes and sizes.

Try to be 1% better by cultivating resilience. When a frustrating situation arises, take a deep breath and figure out how to put a positive spin on it. How can you be resilient in the face of whatever is trying to knock you down? What can you learn from this situation that can help you the next time you encounter a similar situation? Remember, you've survived all of your worst days so far; you are strong enough to get through this one.

Reflection

Resistance

Stop making life more difficult

We resist so much. Actually, we're resisting most of the time whether we know it or not. We resist doing things that we know will make us feel good because we don't want to put in the effort. Or my personal favorite, resisting completing a task that will probably take all of 5-10 minutes just because the thought of doing it creates anxiety for no reason at all (hello, Fellow Procrastinators!).

Why do we do this to ourselves?

It's the usual culprit: our brain. Our brain doesn't like change and discomfort so much that the allure of a reward is often not strong enough to make us do something even if we logically know it's good for us. It seeks out safety and comfort, so why get up and put away clothes when it's so much cozier on the couch watching TV? We are wired for immediate gratification, which becomes its own enabler. When we permit ourselves to give in to immediate gratification, our brain rewards us with a little hit of "happy hormones," so we keep doing the thing that gave us that high, which in turn lets the brain reward us again. Even if I tell my brain I'll feel so much prouder of myself, and relieved once the clothes are put away, it thinks, "But don't you feel good right here right now? Why mess that up?" So, as usual, we are hardwired to be our own biggest enemy.

And over time, this gets heavy and exhausting. There's a reason why exercising with weights is called resistance training. The more we resist something, the heavier it becomes. This is great for building muscle, but not as great when it comes to living life.

When this resistance response kicks in, it's important to remind yourself that you aren't lazy, or failing, or any other adjective you use when you feel resistance. It's just your brain trying to protect you. It doesn't know the version of YOU in the future who will benefit from resolving the resistance. All it knows is the current version of you right now who is currently safe exactly as you are.

So, with this in mind, some ways that we can begin to release areas of resistance in our lives are to first get curious about them. If we know *why* we're resisting, then we can become consciously aware of it, which takes away a little bit of the power from our brains and helps us make more conscious, rational decisions. Overcoming resistance starts from a place of awareness.

What is one area of resistance in your daily life that you dread, and how can you shine a spotlight on it to better understand the *why*? Can you take steps to help relieve that resistance so you can start taking care of Future You? Once you do this, make sure to consciously reaffirm to yourself, "I feel so much better after I do X, Y, and Z. It's worth the extra effort because it makes me feel great." If your mind can hear you say that, over time, it will stop reinforcing resistance against the things you actually want to do.

Reflection

Risks

Go ahead, take the risk

We are wired to avoid taking risks for many of the reasons you've encountered throughout the rest of this book. Our brains like to keep us safe, so they trigger responses that make us avoid taking risks. *But* we are also genetically predisposed to taking different amounts of risk. The way our serotonin and dopamine receptors function as well as the way our prefrontal cortex is constructed play a role in how much risk we're willing to take on and what we even perceive as a risk.

Our environment and learned experiences can also play a role in risk tolerance. For example, if you jumped into the deep end of the pool once, you're likely to feel less risky the next time you do it. And if no one put the idea into your head in the first place that the deep end was scary, then you may not have known it was.

And sometimes we take risks simply because we want attention, while others we avoid risks because we *don't* want the attention if we fail.

In a nutshell, taking risks is a personal experience, but it's one that we all have. While our response to risk can in most cases keep us alive, it can also keep us from living life to the fullest.

When I worked as a freelance writer early in my career, I had to apply to hundreds of publications, and you can probably guess that since I write for none of them currently, that meant receiving hundreds of rejections. That doesn't make me braver than someone who never applies at all, it just means that I don't see that particular failure as a risk where someone else might. And that same person may have no problem cliff diving whereas I have not an ounce of interest in exploring that activity.

But sometimes our aversion to risk does hold us back, and we need to learn to work through it. When we face down the fears inherent in taking a risk we:

- Build resilience
- Boost our confidence
- Learn new skills
- Gain a better perspective on risk
- Open ourselves up to new opportunities

So when you think of risk, think of it twofold: First, acknowledge that whatever your risk tolerance is, it's normal *for you*. We are all created differently, so no two people will see 100% of risks the same. Give yourself that little reminder if you feel like there's something wrong with you just because you don't feel drawn to do the same things other people do. Second, think of what risks really are worth taking and how you can start facing those fears. Can you apply for the job you want even knowing that there's a 50/50 chance you get hired or get rejected? Can you be more outgoing at parties and learn to talk with more people? Can you commit to a goal that seems scary but you know that it will enhance your life experience?

Think of just one risk you can take today. One thing that you can tell your brain, "I know it's scary but the risk is worth the reward if it works out." One thing that has been rolling around in your brain, but you've been too afraid to take the first step. You can do it!

Reflection

Routine

Get more out of your life

I'll be honest, I've never been a fan of routines. Something about them always felt limiting and boring to me. And what's the point of living if it's going to be limiting and boring? But over the past few years, I've completely changed my mind and now try to routinize (not a real word, but you get the idea) as much of my life as possible.

Of all of the ways I've tried to be 1% better, routine has been the most transformative.

It started when I realized how introducing routine into childrens' lives helps ease their anxiety because the kids know what to expect. And routine helps the parents because, as much as is possible with children, they're able to plan their own lives as well. So, I thought why not create a routine for myself as though I was my own parent?

But I quickly found a problem: my "ideal" routine based on what my goals were didn't align with what my actual lifestyle looked like. This led me to play around with my routine and learn a hugely beneficial lesson: routines can change from one day to the next, and from one season of life to the next. If done thoughtfully, routines leave room for experimentation until you find the right mix that works for you. This may mean some days start slower than others and some evenings may look different from the next, but it is possible to find rhythm and harmony within the scheduling confines of each day.

One of the best parts of a routine is that it streamlines your day, leaving you with more energy to think about creative solutions or to just simply relax. For example, if Tuesday is tacos for dinner, then you're done. You don't need to put any more effort into thinking about what you're going to make. How many times have you wasted minutes and sometimes hours deciding what you want to eat? And in the end you end up settling for leftovers, or something you didn't really want in the first place, or nothing at all because it's already late? Here's the thing: just because you have made Taco Tuesday your routine doesn't mean you have to follow it all of the time. If something fun comes up or there's an event you need to go to, then do it! Taco Tuesday will be there for you next week.

Routines like this aren't about making you feel guilty for not adhering to something. They intended to alleviate wasted energy on decision fatigue and resistance while running through those decisions.

The best part is that not only does routine streamline your life and free up energy, there are also real neurological benefits. It reduces your "cognitive load."[61] You also get little hits of dopamine while

---

[61] Donahue, M. Z. (2021, January 11). *The science behind all that "create a routine" advice*. National Geographic.
https://www.nationalgeographic.com/family/article/the-science-behind-create-a-routine-advice-coronavirus

going through your routines, and science shows that those with consistent routines also have improved health.[62]

So, how do you start a routine? There's lots of literature out there about the "right way." You might want to start with a morning routine, making your bed first thing as an easy, early win. Or maybe you want to create a nighttime routine to help you get better sleep. Neither of those worked for me. My mornings and evenings look different on weekdays than weekends which always left me feeling defeated, like I'd failed at routines.

What finally did the trick was choosing one thing I really wanted to make happen, and then adding a few things around that. For example, I like going to bed with clean floors and no dishes in the sink. So, I decided to make that the last thing I consistently did before getting ready to settle into bed. Then, I started to make longer-range routines, like working on my non-fiction writing on Saturdays, my fiction writing on Sundays, and working on my art throughout the workweek when my brain feels a little more drained of words. I prepare meals for 3-4 days at a time (instead of one big 7-day prep like lots of people suggest) because I know that's about as long as I can go without getting bored eating the same thing. Since I gave myself the leeway to get creative with my own routine (vs. making it fit into someone else's "recommended" box) I have been able to successfully adhere to a routine and also feel the

---

[62] Arlinghaus, K. R., & Johnston, C. A. (2018, December 29). *The importance of creating habits and routine*. American journal of lifestyle medicine. https://pmc.ncbi.nlm.nih.gov/articles/PMC6378489/

benefits. Over time, I've added to my routine, but only where it feels right and effortless to do so.

When a routine is right for you, you'll know it.

If you're trying to find more routine in your life, can you start with one new task or action and then build up to more once you find a way to make that task fit comfortably in your life? Can you give yourself permission to try routines your own way in order to reduce your cognitive load? And can you be flexible as you learn more about yourself, what works for you, and what's important to you?

Reflection

Sadness

Sometimes sadness can be helpful

Never in a million years did I think I'd be writing about sadness as a hopeful and helpful topic but here we are.

My friend recently gave me a set of oracle cards, and I drew a pair representing "what to let go of" and "what to bring in more of." I was confused when I drew "happiness" for the former and "sadness" for the latter. Why would anyone release happiness and bring in more sadness? Surely I'd mis-ordered them. But I took it as a sign to dig into the concept of sadness.

So, I thought about it. Do we really need to embrace sadness? Is there a world in which sadness is somehow helpful to us?

When I tell you I was *shocked* to find out there are proven benefits to sadness, I mean I was SHOCKED. It seemed to go against the conventional wisdom about looking on the bright side. But then when I researched the topic, the strength that the side effects of sadness creates started to make sense.

Some benefits of sadness are:[63]

- We build resilience. When we encounter a situation that makes us sad, we need to learn to cope with it to move through that part of our lives. According to one study, "Research indicates the experience of some lifetime

---

[63] Forgas, Joseph, and Steve Hickman. "5 Ways Sadness Is Good for You." *UNSW Sites*, www.unsw.edu.au/news/2017/05/5-ways-sadness-good-you.

adversity predicts lower functional impairment, lower global distress, higher life satisfaction over time, and fewer posttraumatic stress symptoms. Similarly, a moderate number of adverse life experiences is associated with more positive psychophysiological responses and less negative responses to pain."[64]

- We become nicer people with better judgment. Once we've felt sadness, we may feel more compelled to do what is fair and to spend more time giving fairness consideration. It also helps us become less likely to judge other people.
- We can find motivation in sadness. When we are happy, there's no reason for us to stop doing the thing that makes us happy. But if we're sad, it's a signal to the brain that something needs to change and it can motivate us to make those changes.
- We can also improve our memory. In one study, when participants were in a negative mood on a rainy day, their memory recall was sharper than those who were having a good day. This is also partially why we remember upsetting events better than happy ones.

Let me pause and mention that I'm not saying to go out and try to be sad, and if you are feeling depressed, you should definitely seek

---

[64] Seery, Mark D, et al. "Whatever Does Not Kill US: Cumulative Lifetime Adversity, Vulnerability, and Resilience." *Journal of Personality and Social Psychology*, U.S. National Library of Medicine, pubmed.ncbi.nlm.nih.gov/20939649/.

out support. What I'm talking about is the casual sadness we experience here and there.

We all have a friend (or maybe you are the friend) who cries so often that it's nearly on cue. Or maybe you are the opposite and feel guilty about showing emotion. No matter how you are wired, it's important to know that you can and should express your sadness, and that there is a benefit to it.

It's well-documented that ignoring your emotions can lead to an increase in mental health issues, and can also make us feel other emotions like shame just for a totally normal thing like being sad. I tend to do this if I'm sad "over nothing," wondering why I can't get out of the sad funk. But after looking into this subject, I'm now able to greet sadness with more understanding and gratitude.

Sadness helps make us stronger and motivate us to move forward rather than staying in the same place. It can also help us be nicer to others, and there's really no downside to that. How can you feel your sadness 1% more instead of pushing it down or away? And when you do feel sad, can you turn it into some sort of motivating event even if it's just motivating you to understand yourself on a deeper level?

Reflection

Seasons

Everything is just a season

I don't know about you, but winter bums me out. I leave the house as the sun is rising and come home when it sets. For a born-and-raised SoCal girl, that's my nightmare. But I always remind myself that winter is just a season, and soon enough the days will start getting longer and warmer again.

Whether you like winter, summer, spring, or fall, we can learn a lot from the simple fact that they happen. Seasons are inevitable, like the ocean tides. They will come and they will go. And we are along for the ride.

This is similar to how our lives play out. Everything that transpires — whether we find it enjoyable or can't wait for it to end — is a season. And there are lessons to be learned in each of the seasons, even the ones that bum us out. Maybe especially the ones that bum us out!

If you experience a great successful moment in your life, that's awesome! Take the time to stop and celebrate it! While specific successes can't last forever, you can take the time to bask in the seasons when they do. Pat yourself on the back before rushing off to the next thing.

If you're going through a hard time, instead of resenting it, think about what you can learn from it. How can you find something to take away so that your next difficult time isn't so tough thanks to the lessons you learned the first time?

Everything is just a season. Grade school, college, working years, retirement — all seasons. The same way parents don't want their kids to grow up too fast, give yourself the same permission. Don't let your life pass you by because you're trying to rush to the next season.

You will never be this version of yourself again. Take the time to get to know and enjoy the person you are right now at this season in your life.

Last year, my aunt sent me a post about winter. It explained how animals hibernate during this season; they take advantage of the shorter, darker days to hunker down and rest so that they have the energy to make the most of their days during spring and summer. But as humans, we don't focus on that. During the winter holidays, we're all go-go-go. We set goals for the new year and charge ahead full steam when we should be resting, regenerating. It's important to remind ourselves that we are living things and also need seasons of rest.

Whatever you're going through — be it good or bad — it is only for a season.

Why is it important to remind ourselves that even good times are only a season? Because it helps nudge us to stay in the moment and celebrate! Then when the afterglow fades, you aren't upset that the feeling is gone. You know you honored the success during that season.

Can you remind yourself that what you are experiencing is only a season? Whether it's stress, joy, frustration, or satisfaction, you can be 1% better by grounding yourself in the present and knowing that it is all just a season. Lean into the lessons and experiences that will help energize you in the future.

Reflection

Self

There are infinite versions of yourself

If you've ever wondered what people think of you, I have good and bad news. The good news is that everyone thinks something different. The bad news is that everyone thinks something different.

Every person you've ever come across has a different relationship with you, so everyone you've ever met, talked to, strangers who have come across your online profiles, they all hold a different version of you in their head than the next person does. And all of those are different from the image you hold of yourself.

This is cool because it means infinite versions of you exist, but also a little daunting because thanks to a biological need to be liked and accepted by society, it can be tough to swallow that you have to consistently make fresh impressions on people. Or do you...

Why do we try to "be" anything? We have no control over how people see us so why do we try to "be" someone we're not? You could act like the nicest person around someone and they may still walk away thinking, "I don't know, there's just something off. Like she's *too* nice." The point is, why try to "be" anyone when you never leave the same imprint twice AND you really have no control over what that imprint might be.

Every day, we cycle between identities. We are different at work than we are at home than we are with our acquaintances than we are with our close friends… you get the idea.

There are a few theories around this, and the easiest to conceptualize is the four concepts of self-presentation theory. These are:[65]

- Public self
- Self-concept
- Actual or behavioral self
- Ideal self

For your public self, maybe you want to be seen as a leader, as a problem solver, or as a chill vibes person. Or maybe your public self is more complex because you act differently in various social circles; professional by day and the drummer in an underground band by night. Both are public but in different ways. Whatever public self means to you, it's important to realize that it is indeed a bucket of our view of self based on public image.

Which brings us to self-concept. How do you see yourself through your own lens? This one asks us to be honest. Are we too hard on ourselves? Are we taking it too easy? Have we ever stopped to really think about who we are? Despite it seeming simple, I personally find self-concept to be one that feels like

---

[65] Gillette, Hope. "Self Concept: What Is It and How to Form It." *Psych Central*, Psych Central, 12 Apr. 2022, psychcentral.com/health/self-concept#self-concept-theories.

catching smoke. Throughout my life I've been asked to see myself through other people's eyes so often that I never really thought about how I see myself until I was much older. For me, it is an effort to think about "who I am" vs. who I think I am based on the other versions of "self" that I project.

Actual or behavioral self is the showcasing of our actions and habits. I like that it fits between "self-concept" and "ideal self" because this is where thoughts and actions intersect. You can think you are one way, but what are you doing to *actually* be that way? If you want to be a leader, are you actually leading or are you just bossing people around? If you want to be a good friend, do you ask your friends how they are or do you call them and launch into stories about yourself? This is the part of self that holds a mirror up and allows you to take stock of how you show up for your "self" in the world.

Ideal self is who you want to be. What do you want to feel like as you go through life? How do you want to make others feel? What do you want to contribute to the world? What kind of footprint do you want to leave behind? Do you want to be healthier? Wealthier? Wiser? Whatever it is, you can help make your ideal self a reality by putting some of the traits you want into action, bringing it into the circle of actual or behavioral self.

So, how do we find ways to harmonize our public self with our self-concept? And make our actual self take steps towards being our ideal self? It's easier said than done, but the first step is simply to show up as yourself. Find ways that feel safe to you where you can mesh your self-concept with the public.

Finding a balance between your ideal self and your behavioral self is manifestation in action. Manifestation is a buzzword, but it isn't magic. It's the culmination of little acts that add up. If your ideal self is a marathon runner but you don't run, then start by going for a five minute run. Eventually, you'll increase the time and move closer to your ideal self. If your ideal self is a morning person, then start getting up earlier for no reason at all other than you're honoring your ideal self. If your ideal self is less stressed and more relaxed, start practicing mindfulness so that situations aren't as immediately overwhelming.

Everyone is different, so we are all perceived differently by individuals. When someone passes away, we all like to share stories about the person because you learn how many different sides there were to them. That's how we all are. We're all our own little kaleidoscopes who look different to people depending on their interactions with us.

Try to worry 1% less about what others think about you and show up 1% more as your own authentic self. In the end, you don't have a fraction of control over what people think of you, so why not just be yourself and put your energy into being your own personal best self?

Reflection

Self-compassion

Learning to be gentle with ourselves

"You can't say anything worse to me than what I've already said to myself."

I think about this quote a lot. I can't remember where it came from or when I heard it, but it's stuck with me ever since.

We are so hard on ourselves. And often for no reason at all. Few people wake up in the morning and decide, "I'm going to make this the worst day I've ever had. And I'm going to feel terrible at the end of it. Great plan!"

For the most part, we wake up in the morning, earnestly trying to do our best throughout the day. When you choose your best for you, you are quite literally showing up for yourself.

So, when it comes to self-compassion, self-talk is an important factor. It's cliché to say, "Talk to yourself like you would a friend" but it's exactly what you should do. You spend 100% of your life with yourself, no one else. So truly, no one else's opinion of you should matter as long as you are happy with you. And no one else knows your personal struggles like you do. So of all people in this world, you know exactly what you go through and should be most gentle with yourself, right?

But it can be hard to find self-contentment without heaping doses of self-compassion. We mess up. We all mess up every single day.

And learning from those moments is what helps us grow into better versions of ourselves.

There's no need to be cruel to yourself in the meantime though.

This is where the science comes in. Studies show that "Higher levels of self-compassion are linked to increased feelings of happiness, optimism, curiosity and connectedness, as well as decreased anxiety, depression, rumination, and fear of failure."[66] Kind of a "duh" moment, right? If you're nice to yourself, you feel better!

Imagine how much more at-ease you'd be if you went through the day being kind to yourself, allowing yourself to explore, to have awkward interactions, to take a risk.

Try to be 1% nicer to yourself. When you have a self-critical thought, ease up on it and say a nice thing instead. Even something like, "This wasn't as successful as I'd hoped, but I'm proud of myself for trying." That's a million times better than, "What an idiot. I don't know why I thought this would work."

---

[66] Neff, Kristin D. "The Role of Self-Compassion in Development: A Healthier Way to Relate to Oneself." *Human Development*, U.S. National Library of Medicine, June 2009, pmc.ncbi.nlm.nih.gov/articles/PMC2790748/.

Reflection

Self-love

Be the love you crave

"Self-love" is a term that's impossible to escape, but as much as we hear how we all need more of it and how we need to put it into action, self-love is uniquely difficult to understand. That makes it even harder to integrate into our lives.

In doing my research for this topic, I found many tried and true ways to start acting out self-love.[67]

"Speak kindly to yourself," is easy to say, but it is still hard for many of us to integrate into our lives. This is where affirmations can come into play, and the science behind affirmations is pretty cool. Since our brains are malleable, the more we do something, we make that neural pathway clearer for us to do it again in the future. So, if you mess up and choose to be kind to yourself, it'll be easier to be kind the next time, and the next. If you have an unkind thought towards yourself, stop it in its tracks and say something nice. Or use affirmations in a straightforward way by saying several kind things to yourself regardless of the situation.

Empower yourself to be strong. We all fall into ruts where we don't want to do things we know are good for us, but by making ourselves do them, we are making our bodies, minds, and spirits

---

[67] Seppälä Ph.D., Emma. "3 Powerful Science-Based Benefits of a Little Self-Love." *Psychology Today*, Sussex Publishers, www.psychologytoday.com/us/blog/feeling-it/201211/3-powerful-science-based-benefits-little-self-love.

stronger. We are showing ourselves that we love and care for our own wellbeing. Overcoming that resistance is how you show up for yourself. And conversely, sometimes being strong enough to rest when you need to is also showing yourself love and care.

Be your own best friend. I've seen the advice to treat yourself like you would treat a friend, but it wasn't until very recently that I realized I was going through the motions with that. I did all of the things — wrote kind letters to myself (sometimes I actually mailed them, assuming I'd receive the encouragement at the exact time I needed it), giving myself the advice I would give to someone else in my position, seeking the latest research on wellbeing, etc. Then in a meditation class I had a breakthrough. I know I'm hard on myself. I always have been. But in the past I saw it as lovingly parenting myself to achieve more. I never actually figured out how to be my own best friend and simply love me instead of constantly feeling like I needed to guide myself. After that revelation, I've been able to work on being my own confidant, hearing my thoughts without judgment and letting each situation exist exactly as it is.

Self-love is a personal thing. It looks different for each of us. Given the amount of articles, social media posts, podcasts, or books on the topic, one thing is clear: no one is alone in trying to figure out self-love.

The world does not make it easy to know how to love ourselves. People project their own insecurities onto others, and we see that modeled for us at a young age so we do it too. We may even see it from the people we look up to most, the people we want to "be like when we grow up." We hear how adults talk about their own bodies, and think it's okay to talk about ours that way. There are so many ways that the examples of self-love reflected back to us are wrong. They're not the way we should treat ourselves.

So as we grow and mature, it's no wonder that we're confused about what it looks like to unconditionally love and support ourselves. In our busy, go-go-go society, we spend hardly any time trying to understand what loving ourselves looks like.

Here's the great part of all of this though. Yes, self-love is hard. Learning what kind of ways we need to show up for ourselves is hard, but that's okay because there's no one way to do this. Just like all of us are different with our quirks and idiosyncrasies, the way we express self-love is unique.

Try to love yourself 1% more. Look at yourself in the mirror and tell yourself how awesome you are, how you're proud of yourself for facing the day. Do something you know will nourish your body, mind, and soul. Set time aside to relax and read, go to a workout class, get into nature. Whatever it is that you put off or struggle to make time for, prioritize it. Or find something else completely unique to you that will show you how to really love yourself just a little more. You are worth the effort.

Reflection

Self-sabotage

Sometimes you're your own worst enemy

If you're a living, breathing human (so, everyone reading this right now, unless it's 2225 and the robots are for some reason reading a book about how to be 1% better), then you have done something in your life to sabotage yourself. Chances are, you may even sabotage yourself every day in little ways.

Self-sabotage is when we do things that keep us from achieving our goals. Sometimes this is conscious, others we don't even know we're doing it. Sometimes it requires taking an action, while others it means you *didn't* do something.

But why would we do that? Why would we want to keep ourselves from achieving our goals?

Lots of reasons, actually.[68]

It may have to do with something you were told as a child, like, "You'll never be successful," or "People who have too much money are bad people." This becomes a subconscious program in your mind. So, while you want to be successful and wealthy, there's a voice in the back of your head that you may not even be aware of that's guiding you to sabotage those opportunities.

---

[68] Field, B. (2023, November 3). *Why we self-sabotage and how to stop the cycle*. Verywell Mind. https://www.verywellmind.com/why-people-self-sabotage-and-how-to-stop-it-5207635

It may have to do with past wounds. If someone hurt you somewhere along the line then you may avoid situations where that can happen again.

It may have to do with your lived experience. Maybe you want to be a parent, but you came from an abusive household and you're afraid that you'll be that same kind of parent.

Everyone has their own unique relationship with their own self-sabotage and why they do it. So, how can you recognize if it's something that's happening in your own life? Some common ways self-sabotage presents are:

- Procrastination
- Perfectionism
- Self-medication
- Self-criticism

All of these keep us from getting closer to achieving our goals. Procrastination literally puts it off. Perfectionism keeps us so wrapped up in the details that it's nearly impossible to get to the finish line because nothing will ever be perfect. Self-medication can slow us down, and sometimes set us back even further. Self-criticism can take all of the momentum out of our sails, because why do something if we don't even believe in ourselves?

Why do we do all of this? Why don't we just go out there and achieve our goals? It all stems from fear. If you need to overcome a belief that you hold true, then your brain isn't going to like that. New experiences feel like a threat to our conscious brain. It knows what it likes and it wants to stay in the safe "known" space. It reminds me of the saying, "If you want something you've never had, you must be willing to do something you've never done."

Then your next question is likely, "How do I overcome self-sabotage?"

Start by identifying which habits you have that are sabotaging you. Do you undermine yourself at work somehow? Maybe you pass on projects that would get you more visibility. When you're trying to eat a certain way, do you make excuses for yourself to "cheat" on the plan you've chosen? Do you obsess about every last detail of things, sometimes missing deadlines or causing you to disparage what you were working on? Maybe it's as simple as staying up too late when you know you'd be better served by getting a good night of sleep.

We all have decades of stories and programs that we need to unlearn in order to move away from self-sabotage. Today, start small. Commit to identifying one place in your life where you are self-sabotaging and work on that. Do something different than you have in the past in order to move closer to what you want.

Reflection

Service

Making service a way of life

When I was growing up, the modeling I saw for "service" was activities like missions work, volunteering, donating. But as I've gotten older, I've started to wonder what it really means to be of service to people, and are there other ways we can help that go beyond the obvious?

Being of service to people can mean many things. Raising kind kids. Texting people to check on them. Writing letters to friends and family. Being a thoughtful coworker. Donating. Taking care of sick people. Sending a stressed friend $5 for coffee. Helping neighbors with a chore like mowing their lawn. It doesn't have to be big or "one size fits all." You can be of service in small ways.

Service is a word that covers quite a few areas, so let's break them down to find places where we can incorporate daily service into our lives:

Service to ourselves

There's the old phrase, you can't pour from an empty cup. So, think of ways you can be of service to yourself. Can you change something in your schedule to give yourself a little down time? Can you be kind to yourself when you make a mistake? Can you put away savings each month in service to the future-you? Only you know what you need and the good news is that you also have the power to give it to yourself.

Service to others

This is the area where there are lots of suggestions for how to be of service, the most popular of which I've already mentioned, but what else can you do? I like to consider how we can share our gifts. Nearly everyone can volunteer or donate, and they can also make use of their unique talents. Can you offer a free photography session to a young family on a budget? Can you offer to help a friend with home repairs? I give away my books and embroidery patterns if folks are in financial need because I create them specifically to help people unplug and find happiness or an escape for a little while. There are ways to help others all around us if we just think to look for them.

Service to our environment

There are many things we can do to help our environment in small ways every day. Buying from local retailers, picking up trash when you see it, turning off the sink while you're brushing your teeth. The list goes on and on. We all live here. We should want to take care of the place where we live, for ourselves and for others. I guarantee there's a small tweak you can make in your daily life that will better serve the environment.

Service to a higher power

Whatever you believe in, you can do something to serve your higher power that affects people around you in a positive way. Churches of all religions and denominations offer ways to volunteer which helps build community, too. If you don't belong to a church, you can serve in other ways. As a reiki master, I often offer free remote reiki sessions if people need healing, and practice intercessory loving-kindness meditations multiple times a week. Whatever your higher power is, find a way to offer a service here on Earth on behalf of that power.

I hope this helps you think of service differently. And please remember, you can't pour from an empty cup. Don't serve others so much that you forget about yourself. There's only one you, and you can't give your gifts to the world if you aren't energized and whole.

Consider how you can incorporate service into your daily life 1% more. How can you start by serving yourself and then letting that overflowing cup spill out to those around you? Can you leverage your unique talents to make someone else's life better?

Reflection

Shame

Make friends with your shame

In a previous chapter we talked about guilt and now it's time to talk about its close relative, shame. While guilt is a feeling between you and yourself, shame is caused when *other people* make us feel bad. When we do something others don't approve of, it can make us feel ostracized. Since social connections are a huge part of overall wellbeing, this ostracization can be painful. It hurts when we feel like we're in danger of losing those connections! This is why shame can weigh so heavily on us.

Here's the simplified explanation of how the biomechanics work: when we feel shame, the part of our brain that feels arousal is stimulated and the part that powers logical thinking is depressed. This means you're more likely to feel like you need to act on your feelings rather than think them through.

For example, if you share a song you like with a group of friends, but they laugh at you and hate it, chances are you'll have some kind of reaction since shame sends our bodies into fight, flight, or freeze. You may turn the song off immediately, or if you're feeling a little aggressive you may turn it up. But what you're less likely to do is logically think, "I like this song and they don't, and that's okay. Not everyone is going to like the same things." And depending on how you reacted, you may fall into a "shame spiral" where you keep replaying what you did over and over again, ultimately making yourself feel worse.

The process to overcome shame is similar to the process to overcome guilt. Start by accepting that what happened happened and there's nothing you can do to change it. You played a song that they didn't like, and you have to own however you responded to that.

Then the next step — and this is very important! — be kind to yourself. Everyone makes mistakes and you're no different. "To err is human, to forgive is divine," as the famous Alexander Pope quote goes. Rise above whatever the situation was and forgive yourself.

Finally, figure out how to move on. Do you need to apologize to someone who was hurt by your actions? Do you need to simply accept that it happened and let it go? Moving on is crucial, otherwise the moment will continue to live in your mind, and whenever it pops up, you'll cringe and immediately have your mood dampened when you think about the event.

One tip that helps me when I find it hard to forgive and move on is to remember that this is everyone's first rodeo. Even if you believe in reincarnation, this is your first and only incarnation as the person you currently are right now. No one has all of the answers the second we are born, so of course we are going to make mistakes. What matters is that we're able to learn from those mistakes, grow more resilient, and move forward.

To start healing from shame, the next time a moment that triggers this shame response in you pops up, give it the time and space you need to forgive yourself for it and let it go. If you have lifelong close friends or siblings, you know that sooner or later someone will bring up "One time when…" and it may make you feel like you want to die inside. That's why it's so important to address shame on your own time so that those moments affect you less and less as time goes on.

Healing from shame is hard. There may be simple steps, but please know it is hard, and it is something that you will practice for your entire life. So give yourself some grace and love in the process.

Reflection

Sleep

Go to sleep!

Over the past few years, there seems to have been an explosion in getting the message out that good sleep is one of the most important pieces to overall health. We need quality sleep for immune function, metabolism, hormone control, and brain function. And they're making new discoveries about sleep all of the time!

But for many people, sleep feels like this elusive thing. When I got my first sleep tracker, I was showing my score to a friend and she said, "Now we have to worry about being graded on our sleep, too?!" It made me laugh and I think about it a lot, particularly on weeks where my sleep is consistently getting a C grade.

I briefly mentioned all of the ways sleep is beneficial to us, and there are tons of books and podcasts that go into the details so I won't belabor that here. Instead, I want to give you a few things you can try in order to get better sleep, and I want to talk about what happens if you struggle to stay asleep or you sleep *too* deeply.

During the day, well before you're getting ready for bed, you can do things like getting outside into the sunlight in the morning and the afternoon to help your body regulate its circadian rhythms. This is the internal clock that guides your body's actions based on what it thinks you need. If it's winter and you live in a place that only receives a few hours of sunlight every day, you can get lamps that are specialized to mimic the sun. There's no true replacement for our star but these lamps can help. Or, if you're on a budget, just turn on all of your lights in the morning so your body thinks it's daytime and start dimming them or turning them off in the afternoon.

A physically taxing workout is another way to help stimulate quality sleep later in the day. Some studies say that you shouldn't exercise close to bedtime because you will have a boost of energy, but I would encourage you to do what's right for you. When I workout, I tend to go until I'm exhausted, which makes it great an hour or two before I start my nighttime routine. Another tip along these lines is to avoid eating a couple of hours before bed because your body will be working to digest your food and it isn't ready to be in a state of rest if it's still working.

You should also limit when you drink caffeine and alcohol because they can affect your sleep. I find the effect these two chemicals have on our sleep to be fascinating. I'll try to keep it simple but we'll start with caffeine. All day long, a chemical compound called adenosine slowly builds up in our brains and eventually when there's enough, it sends a signal that we need to go to sleep. While we sleep, the adenosine is cleaned out of our brains so we can start fresh when we wake. Caffeine is an adenosine receptor antagonist, meaning that when we drink caffeine, we are inhibiting the signal from adenosine indicating that we are sleepy. So even if you're someone like me who barely feels any effect from caffeine, there are still chemical processes going on in the brain that are being blocked. As for alcohol, despite people thinking they need a nightcap, it's actually going to make sleep worse. Depending on how much and what you're drinking, you may be in for a terrible night of sleep. Similar to eating late at night, when you drink alcohol (or really any sugary, caloric beverage), you're creating work for your body to do, so you're not going to get a good night's sleep. And there's a chance you'll get a sugar spike in the middle of the night that causes you to wake up.

Here are some things you can do before bed to help you get a night of rest. You've heard it a million times but using screens 30 minutes or more before bed can harm your sleep because of the blue light the screens omit. You can get blue light blocking glasses to help with that, but the better solution is to just say no. Establish a sleep schedule and a pre-bedtime routine. This will help your brain get into the rhythm of knowing you're going to bed soon. However, if your workweek schedule differs from your natural body clock, this can be a little tough. I can share what I do, in case it's helpful. During the workweek, I need to be a morning person, but when I let my body tell me when it's tired, I've found that I feel more in-rhythm being awake much later, into the early hours of the morning. That's obviously further apart than the recommended 1 hour difference. So, I've experimented with what feels best in my body and have found a happy medium that works. On weekdays, my sleep score is what it usually is (in the 70s or 80s) because that schedule doesn't feel natural to me, and on weekends I'll often score in the 90s.

Another tip is to keep your room cool. There's some disagreement about the exact temperature it needs to be, but if you aim for 65 degrees, you'll be in good shape. You can also try sleep masks and weighted blankets to help slow down and comfort your nervous system.

And finally, try relaxation techniques. My favorite is to listen to a progressive muscle relaxing meditation, or to listen to yoga nidra. The purpose of yoga nidra isn't specifically to facilitate sleep, but it works so well that I'd feel like I was gatekeeping if I didn't mention it.

Okay, now to answer the question of what to do if you are a light sleeper and struggle to stay asleep or a heavy sleeper and struggle to wake up. I'm sorry to say that some of us are genetically predisposed to be light or heavy sleepers and there's not much we can do to change that. Trust me, this was a blow to me, too. I've always been a light sleeper, so I was hoping to find some silver bullet, but if there is one, it hasn't been discovered yet. The good news is that the field of sleep study is heating up so who knows, maybe there's a discovery on the horizon! In the meantime, just get curious about your sleep. Try some of the tactics in this chapter, and if they don't feel right to you, tweak them to see if they can be beneficial in some other way (like how I find it better to exercise a couple of hours before bed instead of earlier in the day).

This week, just pay attention to your sleeping habits. If you can start implementing some new habits, great. But it's okay to just start by being curious. If you want to learn more about sleep (especially since it's something 100% of us need to do every day), then look up books and podcasts about them. "Why We Sleep" by Matthew Walker is one of the most well known resources on the topic. By the end you'll be convinced that getting better sleep is something worth fighting for.

Reflection

Specialness

Kind words can make a huge difference

When I was a kid, my elementary school was on the other side of my backyard wall. My sisters and I would typically hear the morning school bell ring while we were still in the house getting ready. We'd hurry up, grab our backpacks, and run around the corner to get in our respective class lines, always ending up at the end.

But as we flew out the door, our mom would always yell after us, "Make someone feel special today!" I was a very shy child and found it hard to talk to anybody. So for me, it was a challenge to "make someone feel special." Some days, as the final bell drew near, I'd agonize over how I was going to fit in a special compliment. But I'd do it. Occasionally it was as simple as, "I like your shirt," or, "You did a good job coloring today."

We weren't a family who ate dinner at the table every night — too many extracurriculars for that. But my mom would always follow up with us. "Who did you make feel special today?" and we'd recount what we'd done. There was no punishment if we didn't follow through, she'd just say, "Okay, you can try again tomorrow."

Eventually, making people feel special became a habit more than a directive. Now, compliments flow pretty freely from me. If I like someone's outfit, shoes, whatever, I tell them. If I appreciate someone for even a small act, I tell them. It's not an effort anymore; it's become part of who I am.

My mom passed away from cancer in August '22, but before she did, my sister asked her where she picked up that phrase. Mom shrugged her thin, bony shoulders and said, "Nowhere. I just thought it up."

That was my mom. She treated everyone she met like they were best friends. She made people feel special everywhere she went. She addressed cashiers, mechanics, over-the-phone customer service people by their names. If she wasn't able to catch their name during the conversation, she'd ask before leaving or ending the call so she could personally thank them and wish them a good day.

I think about her directive a lot. "Make someone feel special."

Such a simple but powerful thing.

We always hear phrases like "Smiles are contagious," and, "be kind," but in my opinion there's something about making someone feel special that's slightly different. There's no self-interest in it. Does it feel good to know that you made someone else feel good? Sure, but that's not why you do it. It's purely altruistic. You do it because there is something special about each and every one of us, and we don't tell each other that enough.

I believe that a very simple way to be 1% better each and every day is to flex the muscle of making someone feel special. Edifying and building people up with no agenda. Making it a habit to spread kindness through one simple action.

Comment on a friend's Instagram picture. Tell a coworker you hope they have a great day. Thank your apartment building manager for keeping the place clean. Email your favorite newspaper writer and tell them you like their columns. We are connected to so many people, the options are nearly limitless.

So I'd encourage you to take a few moments and make someone feel special today.

Reflection

Stillness

Cultivating stillness in a constantly moving world

Stillness is my own personal hell. I enjoy a few moments of silence here and there, especially after a day full of meetings or some other long, loud activity… but when I say "silence" I mean silence with a dash of noise. I typically have gentle background jazz or classical music playing at all times. But complete silence — especially long stretches of it — is tough for me.

When I read the book "Stillness is the Key" by Ryan Holiday, it was challenging and compelling in quite a few ways.[69] I won't try to summarize them here (you should definitely read it if you're interested), but I want to talk about the concept of stillness in general.

Stillness gives us space to be ourselves, and in some cases to learn who we are. Stillness frees us from the constantly moving world, with its endless pings, dings, alerts, and activities. Even as I write this, I'm also thinking about the dinner that's cooking on the stove, the text alert that just buzzed on my watch, and the yoga class this evening that I forgot to register for. All of that is far from being still, but it's likely a familiar situation to many of us.

With all of that going on, how can we possibly quiet ourselves down enough to turn inward?

---

[69] Holiday, Ryan. *Stillness Is the Key*. Portfolio/Penguin, an Imprint of Penguin Random House LLC, 2019.

Which brings me to this week's challenge…

What does stillness look like? Well, exactly like what you think it does. But many times we need to be still on purpose.

After I finished "Stillness is the Key," I decided to consciously incorporate stillness into my life. And it is a *grind*. I like to listen to music when I write and meditate. I like to listen to audiobooks and podcasts as often as possible. You will almost never find me without an earbud in one ear. I like to have sports on at least one TV every waking moment. But if I'm doing those things, my mind is never completely still. I'm also a fidgeter and paradoxically nothing makes me fidget quite like being still.

But this week I sought out opportunities to be still. I went to the beach and laid there with no music on, just listening to the sounds of the waves, letting my mind be free. It was nice… for about five minutes. Then I wanted music and a book to read. I went to a yoga class where the teacher happened to not play any music in class. Though my body was moving, my mind was challenged to be still and keep my breath without a background sound to anchor on. So, it hasn't been a great success pursuing stillness in my life but I am going to continue trying. The benefits are too great and necessary not to!

To be 1% better, try to continue to consciously seek out opportunities to be still. To stop what you're doing and take a few deep, smooth breaths when you're starting to feel stressed or are overthinking. To not respond to texts and emails the second they come in. To ask yourself, "Is this actually urgent?" To simply stop and take in your surroundings.

Reflection

Storytelling

Whether you realize it or not, you're a storyteller

Earlier in the book, we talked about mind reading. Well, I like to think of storytelling as mind reading's other half. Mind reading is something you do internally, wondering how people see you or what they think of you, you're monitoring the mood of every room you're in. Storytelling is the outward projection of that.

It's important to remember that our brains are always trying to keep us safe. We may be very smart, but at our core we're still animals with one overarching goal: stay alive. And that's why anxiety is helpful. But it's also why we make things up all of the time.

Picture this: you're at the store and you see a woman staring at an item on the shelf. You have no idea what she's doing. Maybe she's zoned out, maybe she's deciding if she wants to buy the item. You'll never know what she's doing, but your brain will make up a story to help assess any potential threat and keep you safe.

Or maybe you see two men yelling at each other. Your instinct is to stay away because you think they may be about to fight. But then you realize they are laughing and embracing. Through eavesdropping you overhear they're longtime friends who haven't seen each other in ages. The yelling was how they expressed excitement. But your brain tried to keep you safe and created a story that there was danger ahead.

Sometimes our storytelling gets nasty if we aren't aware of our own implicit biases. There are way too many stories of parents who look like they are a different race or have a different last name than their children, and are summarily accused of kidnapping by people who spun up a narrative in their own heads.

So, now that we know why storytelling can be neutral, helpful, or hurtful, let's explore a tiny bit more.

Storytelling isn't just a way to keep us safe — Our brains love stories! They help us feel more connected and broaden our personal frame of reference. There's actually a mounting pile of evidence surrounding how stories make us feel.

So, how do we stop storytelling? We have to first become aware of it. I like to practice this on my daily walks. Whenever I see someone and start to make up some story about them in my head. "They look happy. Probably listening to a great song," or "Woah, that person is having a bad day," or something else based on how they are acting.

When these scenarios arise, I stop myself. I haven't a single clue who that person is or what's going on with them. Nor do I need to. I can just observe the situation and keep it moving.

Sometimes when we're in a generally negative mindset, that can color our stories and give us a bleak outlook on life. And when we have a positive one, it's possible we can be too trusting in situations where we shouldn't.

So be mindful of the situation, but don't let your mind race ahead of you. Then you can move on with whatever it is you were doing.

Observe the stories you start to tell yourself so you can gain insight into your own mental state. Try to catch yourself 1% more of the time when you're storytelling. Then stop the story and passively watch it play out instead.

Reflection

Surrender

Let go

For the past few weeks, I've been getting the same message over and over again: surrender. In yoga class, on a podcast, on a homemade sign over the freeway, "SURRENDER" has been coming through loud and clear. The concept of surrender isn't an easy one for me. I like to plan and prepare, typically coming up with a Plan A to Plan C. Then once I've thought through all of the details, I can sit back and let one of the plans fall into place.

But lately I've been finding myself in situations where I'm powerless. Whether it's something at work, a project that isn't going as planned, or any of the other things that can go awry in a day. I used the word "powerless" on purpose because it can feel like that when power, or control, is taken away. But I started thinking about it in a different light. What if I intentionally surrendered to the situation?

The more I thought about surrender, the more I thought about how it's a cornerstone of all major religions. In theistic religions you surrender to a higher power. In nontheistic religions, you surrender to being, existing. In philosophy, the Stoics, Existentialists, and many others espouse the idea that we have no real control, so don't worry. Brene Brown unpacks it well:

"Surrender is not about giving up, but about letting go of counterfeit control."

You may have heard the saying, "Man plans, and God laughs." That's speaking to counterfeit control. When we think we've got something buttoned up, that's just counterfeit control. Any number of things can change in a second.

Eckhart Tolle also has some wisdom about this: "Surrender is the simple but profound wisdom of yielding to rather than opposing the flow of life." Resistance is heavy, surrender is light.

How can you train yourself to surrender 1% more of the time? Where can you let go of counterfeit control? Can you make the conscious choice to go with the flow?

Reflection

Time

Time really does fly when you're having fun

Have you ever noticed that occasionally time seems to be dragging for everyone you talk to? Or a day seems to fly by? Well, what if I told you that time actually does speed up or slow down depending on what you're doing.

Not to get too physics-y here, but time doesn't happen in a straight line. That's just how we experience it. Time is always happening all around us. And science can measure how we experience the passing of time.

An article in the National Library of Medicine explains:[70]

"Unexpectedly pleasurable events boost dopamine release, which should cause your internal clock to run faster. Your subjective sense of time in that case grows faster than time itself, so short intervals seem longer than they are."

This immediately made me think of football, or sports in general. For me, a three or four hour game can feel like it was maybe only one or two hours long because it's full of unexpected enjoyable events. But for someone who doesn't like sports, it can feel much, much longer since the events don't bring them any joy.

---

[70] Simen, Patrick, and Matthew Matell. "Why Does Time Seem to Fly When We're Having Fun?" *U.S. National Library of Medicine*, U.S. National Library of Medicine, 9 Dec. 2016, pmc.ncbi.nlm.nih.gov/articles/PMC6042233/.

Time is different for all of us in different contexts. Studies show that our automatic timing is controlled by the cerebellum and is responsible for tracking milliseconds.[71] Our cognitively controlled timing is in the prefrontal areas of the brain and tracks minutes. So your brain automatically does things in milliseconds, then in minutes starts to process what's happening. For example, your body is automatically breathing right now. Then your brain becomes aware that your body is breathing. Those happened on two different scales of time (automatically and cognitively).

Our emotional state can affect how we view time passing as well.[72] If you are happy, time may still move "slow" but if you're excited and pursuing a goal, it may move "fast." Time flies when you're having fun, right? Then there are other emotional and cognitive states like the "flow" state. This is when you're engaged in a mentally stimulating activity that could go on for hours and you'd have no idea that much time passed because your brain is so wholly engaged in what you're doing.

The speed with which we perceive time passing is also affected by our age. A paper by Professor Adrian Bejan in the European Review explains the neurological reasons why, but here's the gist: when you are younger, you're processing more images because

---

[71] Fontes, Rhailana, et al. "Time Perception Mechanisms at Central Nervous System." *Neurology International*, U.S. National Library of Medicine, 1 Apr. 2016, pmc.ncbi.nlm.nih.gov/articles/PMC4830363/.

[72] Dawson, Joe, and Joe Sleek. "The Fluidity of Time: Scientists Uncover How Emotions Alter Time Perception." *Association for Psychological Science - APS*, 28 Sept. 2018, www.psychologicalscience.org/observer/the-fluidity-of-time.

your brain is growing.[73] As we age, brain growth slows and we process less. Additionally, we see less "new" things as we age which can make them less remarkable to our brains. Think about the first time you drove a car compared to the 475th time you drove a car. You likely have a vivid memory of the time you first drove but can't even begin to remember the 475th time. That's because over time, it became more common and less memorable.

I used to anecdotally think about this when I was 16 years old and working at In-N-Out Burger. A four-hour shift seemed like the longest shift in the world. I couldn't fathom how people did an eight hour shift. Then I thought back to school breaks as a kid and how they seemed to last forever, but as I got older, each summer seemed to go by faster and faster.

When you are young, each day is fractionally larger than a day will be later on. One day in a one-year-old baby's life is 1/365th of their life. One day in a 30-year-old's life is 1/10,950 of their life. That's a significantly smaller fraction of life than it is for the baby.

So there are many reasons why it feels like time passes slow or fast, or why vacations never seem as long as they used to the older you get. But that highlights why it's even more important to make every day matter.

I frequently think of an idea I once heard. You don't have to make every day your best day. But rather, live each day in a way that if

---

[73] Bejan, Adrian. "Why the Days Seem Shorter as We Get Older: European Review." *Cambridge Core*, Cambridge University Press, 18 Mar. 2019, www.cambridge.org/core/journals/european-review/article/why-the-days-seem-shorter-as-we-get-older/2CB8EC9B0B30537230C7442B826E42F1.

you had to repeat it for the rest of your life, you'd be OK with that. We have obligations, work, life maintenance stuff. Not every day can be a "perfect" day, but days can be the best you can make of them. A life is made up of tens of thousands of days, and each one helps complete the picture of the life you led.

Try to be 1% better by simply observing the passage of time and making tweaks to enjoy it more. If a day is dragging on, that's an indicator that you're missing out on some good vibes. So find a way to make it fun. If time is going fast, try to be consciously present for more of the moments. What are some ways you can get control of your time to live your fullest life?

Reflection

Today

Just for today

I don't know about you, but I spend a lot of time thinking about the future. I like to plan my projects, assign deadlines, train for races, etc. But thinking that way often gets overwhelming and occasionally I burnout or shutdown.

During my reiki training, I learned the reiki precepts, which are said at the beginning of every day:

Just for today, I will not be angry.

Just for today, I will not worry.

Just for today, I will be grateful.

Just for today, I will do all my life's work honestly.

Just for today, I will be kind to all living things.

That's only five statements, but if you think about them on their own, it's actually kind of a tall ask. Don't get angry? Don't worry? Be kind to *all* living things (including *yourself*)? I don't know about you, but the second I'm inconvenienced, these three commitments become instantly challenged.

Imagine you're in line at the local cafe. You're not running late for work, but you have exactly seven minutes to get in and out of there. However, you're in line behind someone who has apparently never ordered coffee before. They ask all kinds of questions about lattes and cappuccinos and what the various milks do to the various drinks. You now only have four minutes to get out of there, you haven't ordered, and there's a queue of drinks they need to make in front of yours. You think about leaving, but finally, you're at the front of the line. You place your order, but you're frustrated with the person in front of you (who was probably just having a nice time learning about coffee), you're worried about being late, you are likely feeling stressed instead of grateful.

You can see how all of these principles work together with each other and how easily it is for one little decision to derail you.

In the recovery community there's a frequently used phrase, "One day at a time," because it's too hard to think about never doing something again, and that often sends people back into relapse. This is also why people tend to fail at diets. It feels like too big of an ask to do something/not do something for X amount of days let alone forever. Or why after a diet, some people go right back to their old ways because it was only ever meant to be a short-term commitment.

That's why I love the concept of "today." We all know tomorrow isn't promised, so why do we spend so much time thinking about it?

What can you do or tell yourself today to help take some of the pressure off tomorrow while also helping you live your best life today? Can you welcome more grace for others into your life today? Can you commit to going to being a healthier version of yourself "just for today? Can you choose to not worry about anything that is stressing you out if it isn't aligned with what you need to get done *today*?

It's hard. In part, it's hard because our brains become addicted to worrying. It gives them something to do when everything is otherwise going well. But today, try to take 1% off your mental plate if it isn't serving your goals for that particular day. And if you aren't sure where to start, try the reiki precepts or choose your own five statements. You don't need to be a practitioner to reap the benefits of incorporating them into your everyday life.

Reflection

Trauma

We are all traumatized

I have often found that when the concept of trauma comes up, people tend to think that it only pertains to those who have gone through some serious shit in their lifetimes. But that isn't the case. We *all* have trauma in our past and it's important to acknowledge it so that we can heal and begin to move forward.

Trauma can come from a bad breakup, bullies at school, moving to a new city, or even starting a new job. If an event is causing you to feel overwhelmed in your thoughts, feelings, or in your body, then that is trauma.

When I was 11 years old, my aunt and five cousins were killed instantly in a car accident. For *years*, I was convinced that if anyone left our house, they were going to die and I'd never see them again. To this day, I tell people to text me and let me know they got home and if they don't, I check in to make sure they're safe. This is a trauma I live with all of the time.

The good news is that there's been a lot of research done in the world of trauma and there are tons of tools people can use to help them with theirs. Therapy is an obvious one, though the cost may be prohibitive for many people, so I want to share other healing modalities that may be able to help.

Somatic therapy is a little hard to grasp because it's very individual, but it boils down to moving your body to get the energy flowing instead of being stuck. Think about how you feel when anxiety, fear, or depression descends on you. Chances are there's tightness in your body somewhere, so somatics helps encourage you to move your body in an effort to alleviate that tension. Think of it this way: If you ball your hand into a fist then extend your fingers, you have to move your hand in order to release the tension.

A style of meditation called EFT (Emotional Freedom Tapping) has also become more popular in recent years. This involves tapping on various meridians of your body to help calm the nervous system. Some versions also involve speaking aloud to remind your brain that you are safe and there is no threat.

You can journal. As mentioned previously, I'm not a big journaler, but I found that it was one of the only ways I was able to heal from a specific event that caused significant PTSD in my life. In forcing myself to relive the incident in detail, I was signaling to my brain that it wasn't something I needed to push down, that it was part of my life, it was over, and it was safe to acknowledge both of those aspects.

We are all carrying trauma, and I would be remiss if I didn't recommend the book "The Body Keeps the Score" by Bessel van der Kolk here. But if you don't have the time or desire to read an entire book on trauma, then I hope you've been able to find some tools to help you here.

Now, for the 1% better part of this... Can you give yourself the grace to acknowledge that no matter the severity of your trauma, it is valid and you are worthy of healing? And can you take one step towards that healing journey? Whether it's looking up some kind of EFT meditation on YouTube, finally taking the leap to talk with a therapist, or just going outside to take a walk in nature and reset, you deserve to heal.

Reflection

Trust

You know best

Fun fact: You have lived 100% of your life with yourself, so you know 100% of what you have done and are capable of so far. That's an unparalleled data sample size! And yet, with all of that in mind, people still struggle to trust themselves to make the right decision.

Think about a time when you made a "bad" decision, or one where a situation didn't work out the way you'd hoped. If you're sitting here reading this, you made some subsequent decisions that got you out of the situation. So, in the end, maybe your first decision didn't pan out exactly like you'd planned, but a collection of the next decisions you made did.

In her book "Thinking in Bets," author and professional poker player Annie Duke explains decision making.[74] When looking at two poker hands, she explained that one would win 76% of the time and the other would win 24% of the time. She bet on the hand that won 76% of the time, but in this case the second hand won. Everyone started telling Annie she got it wrong. But Annie explained it wasn't wrong, it was simply going to be right 24% of the time, and this was one of those times.

---

[74] Duke, Annie. *Thinking in Bets: Making Smarter Decisions When You Don't Have All the Facts*. Portfolio/Penguin, 2019.

When we make decisions for ourselves, we tend to think of them in terms of right and wrong, but really they're just choosing one thing over the other, and adapting from there.

While it's important to understand what drives our decisions, it's equally important to trust ourselves that no matter what decision we make, we'll figure out what happens next.

Trusting your gut or intuition is rooted within you. You really do know best. How many times have you made a decision, then changed your mind to a more familiar, comfortable choice that ended up making your life harder?

You choose to stay in a boring relationship because it's better to stick with what you know. Or you don't start a home improvement project because what if you mess up? Or you don't join a local group because what if they don't like you? The scenarios are almost endless. And yes, other adjacent concepts are at play here. Things like self-doubt and imposter syndrome, but in my opinion, trusting your gut is the most basic building block. If you trust yourself, other things fall into place.

So how do we work on trusting ourselves? I'll be honest, I second guess myself all of the time. I'm a classic overthinker to the point I often have analysis paralysis. It's less that I doubt myself and more that I go over all of the options available to me until I think myself right out of a good decision. Luckily, there are plenty of tactics to learn from.

One concept that's helpful in learning to trust your gut is to reframe "right" and "wrong." If you choose to stay up late instead of going to bed early, you might be tired in the morning, but that doesn't mean it was "wrong." It's just something you can learn from in the future.

Another tip is to set an achievable goal. If you don't trust your gut because you feel like you always get it wrong or fail, then set yourself up for success. Set a goal you can reach, like drinking a glass of water first thing in the morning for a month. Once you prove to yourself you can do these things, you'll trust yourself more.

Identify your strengths and build on them. If you know you're good at public speaking but lack the opportunity, join a local Toastmasters chapter. If you are good at cooking, write down and share your own personal recipes. The more you show up for yourself, the more you trust yourself.

Quit second-guessing. Make a decision and stick to it. If it's a long-term decision like starting a business, you can certainly pivot based on new information — always be flexible — but believe in each decision you make as you make it. You came to that conclusion for a reason. Trust in how you arrived at it. Think back to when you took tests in school and they'd tell you to go with your first inclination as the answer. Go with your gut.

Start to be 1% better by trusting yourself. Everyone's relationship with themself is different. So find places where you can strengthen yours. Show up for yourself simply by believing in your ability to do the best thing for you, whatever that may look like.

Reflection

Unplug

Gentle ways to help you put the phone down

The encouragement to "unplug" is everywhere. And as annoying as it is, it's with good reason.

There are stacks of data to show that the time we spend on-call to check alerts on our phones has long-term detrimental effects on our mental and physical health. As humans, we need a natural level of anxiety to survive, but the mere sound of our phone can trigger a fight, flight, or freeze response.[75] Your body doesn't immediately know the difference between a threat and a phone notification. The brain has to assess the context of the ALERT, but in the meantime that anxiety response gets kicked into gear. Every time you get an alert there's a potential for your body to have this response. That's a lot of stress over the span of a life.

About five years ago I turned off all notifications on my phone except for staples: texts, calls, calendar alerts. I noticed near-immediate changes in my wellbeing. I checked social media way less because there wasn't anything encouraging me to check in at all times of the day and night. I also felt less on-call to respond to messages the second they arrived. In general, I was interacting with my phone less and staying present more.

---

[75] Team, The Healthline Editorial. "How to Recognize the Causes of Stress." *Healthline,* Healthline Media, 29 Mar. 2020, www.healthline.com/health/stress-causes.

But is it possible to ever FULLY unplug? Personally, I don't think that is a super responsible way to go about life. I think you should check in with your phone at least once a day in case there is some kind of emergency. It's no different than when we had landlines and answering machines you could dial into and hear your messages. Or before those, if you went on vacation, you'd let your friends and family know where you were staying in case they wanted to reach you.

That said, I do think there are a few steps you can take to get closer to feeling less on-call which is what triggers the fight, flight, or freeze.

Acknowledge that your nervous system is currently accustomed to the constant pings. So start by turning off non-essential notifications. Or go a step further and put your phone on silent. You may feel immediate relief like I did, but you may also feel a type of sadness as your brain starts to understand, "It's not that no one is talking to me. It's that I'm making space for myself."

Get a smartwatch that will tell you when you have texts or calls so that you don't have to pick up the phone to look (preferably one that doesn't allow you to respond so you aren't tempted to do so). Once the phone is in your hand, your habits will take over and you'll be tapping into your socials in no time. You can get smartwatches and fitness trackers for as cheap as $40. When I got one of these, it freed me up to leave my phone in the other room and only check in if I got a text or call that actually needed answering. It helps break the need to immediately respond simply because your phone isn't with you.

Along those lines, leave your phone in another room as much as you can. If you're really struggling to disconnect, please know that's normal and you're far from alone. Little exercises like physically detaching from your phone can help break the cycle. If you're watching TV, put your phone in another room and commit to leaving it there for the entire episode. This will help break you of doomscrolling, which fractures your attention and harms your mental wellbeing.

Commit to only checking in with the news once or twice a day. I recently tried this as part of a digital detox for 10 days and I felt so good that the habit stuck. Instead of seeking to stay "up to date" on everything, I chose not to. I listened to a quick 15 minute news podcast in the morning and one at night so that I knew the headlines of the day, but that was it. Whenever I get caught up in the news cycle again, I can physically feel how much it stresses me out. So if you're able to, I highly recommend trying to limit your time with the news. It was incredible how much space it made in my day to listen to entertaining podcasts, audiobooks, and anything else that made me feel uplifted instead of mired in the muckraking.

There are entire books written about unplugging, so I'll stop there. But these are four easily actionable things you can do today that will make an immediate improvement in your mental health. You don't have to do all of them; start with one that you think is helpful and go from there. This is a super impactful way to be 1%

better that will reap decades of rewards for your mind and body. Give it a try!

Reflection

Urgency

Urgency can't be the norm

There's a Lao Tzu quote that goes, "Nature does not hurry, yet everything is accomplished."

The image of a redwood, a majestic oak tree, or a saguaro cactus come to mind every time I read this quote. These impressive plants are famous for their size and the sometimes hundreds of years they have been alive. They've been through wars, famines, droughts, and floods, slowly growing, inching their way towards the sky every year.

There's nothing they need to do except exist and they still grow.

What would our lives look like if we adopted the concept of slow, steady, inevitable growth?

Unfortunately, that's not exactly realistic in our highly connected world where everything seems so urgent. If you don't answer someone's IM or email, they text you. If you don't answer the text, they call you. And I'd bet that most of the time, what was urgent to them is not actually urgent.

While thinking about this, I laughed at the memory of what my mom called "30 minutes in Macy's." With four kids, we often needed stuff for school. Outfits for a spirit day, shoes, or maybe a new shirt just because we wanted it. The point was we all had busy schedules — sports, homework, theater productions — so if we wanted to get what we needed, it had to be fast. We'd pull up to the Macy's department store at the mall, then split up, and meet back together at the register 30 minutes later.

Today, as an adult with an ever-growing "to do" list that would take several lifetimes to finish, I understand where her urgency came from… but I also understand it's not constantly necessary. And I'm sure you already know or have guessed that urgency has harmful health effects, from increased adrenal hormones to higher blood pressure.[76]

Constantly being in a hurry can kill you faster.

This doesn't mean to throw your "to do" list out the window or have no plan. But rather reassess what is actually "urgent."

Chances are pretty good that if I can't do something right this second, there won't be significant negative consequences. If I don't get around to dusting today because I was doing an activity I enjoy, that's okay. The world won't end. If my run is a little slower than normal, that's fine. I don't need to always beat my time. If I'm home a little later because I was enjoying a chat with a friend, no big deal.

A lot of the time, we create urgency in our heads. Not all of the time. Some things truly are urgent. But if everything becomes urgent, then how can we understand true urgency? We are like "the boy who cried wolf" to ourselves until rushing from one thing to

---

[76] Alley, William D. "Hypertensive Urgency." *U.S. National Library of Medicine,* U.S. National Library of Medicine, 4 Sept. 2023, www.ncbi.nlm.nih.gov/books/NBK513351/.

the next is the norm. And that can't happen. For our physical and mental wellbeing, urgency can't be the norm.

Start questioning urgency 1% more when the feeling creeps in. Stop your train of thought and ask yourself, "Is this actually urgent?" And if it's not, then don't worry about it. If it matters, you'll get around to it. Remember, "Nature does not hurry, yet everything is accomplished." You are also a part of nature. You are a living, breathing being and you weren't put on this planet to rush through life.

Reflection

Vibrations

Feel your own energy

I know this theme sounds a little "woo-woo" but if you'll humor me for 10 seconds, try this. Rub your hands together as fast as you can and count to 10, then stop. Notice what your hands feel like. Can you feel them vibrating a little more noticeably than before? You can do this exercise any time to remind yourself that there is always energy flowing through you at different vibrations.

Think about listening to loud music and how you'd feel differently if the music were scream-o music or if it was a calm harp playing. The different styles would change the vibrations in your body to match their output.

Why does this matter? We are all born with our own unique vibrational frequency. That's why some people you meet are always bouncing off the walls and others are more subdued. Neither is better nor worse than the other, they're just different.

This is true on a molecular level. The molecules need to vibrate at complementary frequencies in order to merge or repel. These vibrations, based on the makeup of the molecules, is what creates the chemical reaction. There have even been some Energy Medicine studies that show a connection between a person's vibration and treatment of diseases like cancer, Parkinson's disease, Alzheimer's disease, multiple sclerosis, and more.[77]

So, how does being aware of the fact that we are always vibrating to the beat of our own drum help us be 1% better? First, it helps strip away the curse of comparison. You are, to your core, different from anyone else. So when you feel like you are "too much," or you can't keep up with other people, or whatever it is, remember that's not true because you're just being yourself and that's awesome! Second, it's going to help you get back in touch with how you ideally want and need to feel. If you're doing an activity and it feels "off," then stop, take a few breaths and ask yourself what would feel good right now? One thing I like to do is carve out one day or at least half a day every two-ish weeks where I have no obligations. I just wake up and go through the day doing only what feels right in each moment. Strangely, I find that I'm more active, creative, and productive on those days, even though my goal is to go through the day with as much ease as possible. It reminds me of the activities that make me feel alive and happy.

How can you get more in touch with your own personal vibration today? How can you find opportunities to do things that light you up and make you feel like the happiest, healthiest, best version of yourself (whatever "best" means to you)? And at the very least, can you gently remind yourself that you are a unique vibrational being

---

[77] French, M. (2024, September 23). *What is vibrational energy? definition, benefits, and more.* Healthline. https://www.healthline.com/health/vibrational-energy#health-and-vibrations

and there is no one else on Earth like you, so it's okay to be yourself.

Reflection

Vulnerability

Being vulnerable is courageous

In recent years, there has been an explosion of research about the importance of being vulnerable. As humans, we are both consciously and subconsciously trying to keep ourselves safe. But many times that means that we miss out on opportunities to genuinely connect with other people.

Embracing vulnerability doesn't mean laying your whole being bare to everyone you meet. That would be a little *too* much. But being vulnerable does mean sharing parts of yourself that you feel comfortable sharing with people who you genuinely want to make connections with. And that takes some bravery because no one wants to feel rejected, especially after being very honest and open with someone.

The benefits of being vulnerable can be vast. It can help us build deeper connections with people and help us understand how better to work and live with people. If you explain, "I react this way because of X," it helps other people understand you a little more. If you were around a lot of yelling as a child, maybe you start to feel a little panicked when people near you start yelling, even if it's good naturedly. By being vulnerable about that, you allow your friends to support you in those situations.

My favorite thing about vulnerability is that you get to choose how much you disclose. For example, if you're talking with a narcissist, being vulnerable could mean exposing yourself to potential attacks from them in the future. So, it's not a great idea to be fully open and vulnerable to the entire world all of the time. Always remember that you have full control over how vulnerable you want to get and you can go at your own pace.

Is there a part of your life that could benefit from 1% more vulnerability? It could even be your connection with yourself if there's an issue you've been avoiding thinking about. Remember: vulnerability increases our ability to connect, which in turn can enrich our life experiences. It isn't weak to be vulnerable; it's one of the most courageous things you can do.

Reflection

Whimsy

Seeking fun in the moment

So far in this book, I've touched on the importance of creativity, play, and other concepts that may seem like synonyms for "whimsy," but there's one additional factor that whimsy brings to the plate. Whimsy is acting on the creative or playful urges… on a whim!

Have you ever just felt like getting up and dancing? How would you feel if you dropped everything and went along with that urge? We do this in some ways, like going out for a walk if we feel the need, but a walk isn't exactly whimsical.

I loved the movie *Milo and Otis* when I was a kid and one of my favorite parts was when Milo (the cat) is out in a field and encounters a baby deer. The fawn shows Milo how to "bound and leap" and within seconds, Milo follows its lead, announcing "I'm frolicking! I'm frolicking!" That's the spirit of whimsy. Milo didn't think, "Well, now I've seen how it's done. I'll give it a go later." He just went ahead and tried to bound and leap.

I realize that we all have responsibilities and can't give in to every urge of whimsy that we might have, but what if we gave in just a little more often? The next time you're doing dishes and feel the need to stop and have a mini-dance party, do it! Or when you drive past the same store every day, thinking, "I really want to stop in there sometime," just stop and do it.

Whimsy doesn't have to be this big creative act, it's just giving in to small moments of curiosity and seeing where they lead. You don't need to abandon all of your plans for the day, just allow yourself 5-10 minutes to do something that feels fun to you.

Life is busy and we all go through periods where it feels like tragic events are relentless, so why not make it a practice to identify and honor these small moments of joy, this feeling of whimsy? By now you know that you're largely in control of how your neural pathways form and how to condition positive thoughts to come to you. This can be the same for whimsy. You can train your brain to quickly see opportunities for something that might make you feel more joyful and more free. Start acting on them 1% more of the time and see how you feel.

Reflection

Wins

Set yourself up for success

When it's time for me to leave the office for the day, going to the kitchen and washing out my coffee cup is often the last thing on my mind. Which means I start the next day with a chore: washing my cup from the previous day… Something I very easily could have done before I left in the afternoon.

One morning while I was washing my cup, I was chatting with a coworker. I joked, "It's like the 'make your bed' of office life. I leave the dirty cup so I can start the day with a small win by washing it." Then me being me, I immediately chastised myself, "One day I'll be the person who washes their cup before leaving, but that clearly wasn't yesterday."

The man I was talking to responded, "No! You are right. We all need small, early wins in the day. So keep on washing that cup in the morning."

I thought about it and said, "You're right. I was joking before, but it's actually true."

For those who don't know what I mean by "Make your bed," you should read the bestseller about it.[78] But the gist is that by making

---

[78] McRaven, William H. *Make Your Bed: Little Things That Can Change Your Life --and Maybe the World*. Grand Central Publishing, 2017.

your bed, you're already setting an accomplished, ambitious tone for your day.

I know this might sound anecdotal or silly, but there's science behind it. When you check something off your "to do" list, your brain gives you a hit of that sweet, sweet dopamine.[79] You literally feel happier. That's why some people can't quit their "to do" lists. Some friends and I have even confessed to each other that after we do a task that wasn't on the list, we write it on just so that we can also check it off.

Think about how you can set up other parts of your life for small wins. Instead of going nuts trying to check off everything on your "to do" list before you go to bed, is there some small task or chore you can set aside to start with a small win? For many of us, it's not even a matter of procrastination. It really is a lack of time to get everything done and still be able to take care of ourselves.

And it doesn't just have to be in the morning! Look for ways to find small wins throughout the day, even if it means doing something counterintuitive like leaving a cup unwashed in the afternoon.

I hope this helps set you up for a lifetime of small wins!

---

[79] Sawhney, Vasundhara. "Why We Continue to Rely on (and Love) to-Do Lists." *Harvard Business Review,* 27 July 2023, hbr.org/2022/01/why-we-continue-to-rely-on-and-love-to-do-lists.

Reflection

Words

Words are your greatest power

Did you know that the words that we say, hear, and think have an effect on many parts of our brains, including the frontal lobe (cognitive reasoning), parietal lobe (compassion and empathy, especially to the self), amygdala (processing emotions, including fear and anxiety), and prefrontal cortex (executive functions). There's a *lot* of science to dig into there, but since this isn't a textbook, I'll leave it for now and focus on the bottom line: words have a powerful effect on us which is important when you think about all of the ways you engage with words every day. You're doing it right now! You're reading words, your thoughts are words, you speak and text words, you listen to words through music, films, TV, social media. Words are inescapable. It's no wonder that people struggle the first few days when they embark on a silent retreat!

Since words are inescapable, we have the wonderful opportunity to make them work to our advantage. We can choose to listen to things that make us feel good, or say things that uplift ourselves and others. When we speak or write words, they have a reinforcing effect of us putting them out into the world, and then hearing or reading them back to us.

In our brains, the difference between other people and ourselves is not "fixed," which means that sometimes, when we are talking or thinking about others, our brains will think it applies to us. So when you critique someone else, there's a real chance that your brain is going to think it applies to *you* and will respond accordingly. Or when you read a book, your brain spends so much time engaging with the characters that sometimes it doesn't know they're not real people. That's why finishing a book can feel so painful. Cognitively, these characters are people you have grown to know intimately and will never "see" again.

Full disclosure, I'm currently researching a new book called "The Power of Words" because once I started looking into this topic, I was blown away by how truly powerful our words are. That means I can go on and on with example after example, but for now, let's just talk about small, actionable ways that you can use the power of words to help you make your life better right now.

The first may seem obvious but it's simply to be nicer to yourself. Back when I was having massive anxiety attacks, I made it a point to challenge every single anxious thought I had. When I'd worry about a situation at work, I'd think to myself, "I tried my best and I'm proud of myself for that." In these moments, a simple reminder like "I am safe" can be a powerful tool as well. If you're self-critical, try halting those thoughts and make yourself think something positive instead. It sounds corny, I know, but it's a super simple tactic that really does make a difference. You can also try intaking more words that amplify what you want in your life. Listen to songs with a positive message every once in awhile (Snoop Dogg's *Affirmations* is a go-to when I absolutely can't pull myself out of a funk), or watch a movie that makes you laugh and feel good, or read a book that can help you get into a more constructive mindset.

There's a reason I'm ending the 100 simple ways to be 1% better with a section on words, and it's not just because it starts with W. It's because your words can support you in any other of these situations. Of everything you can do to help yourself, paying attention to the words you take in and put out is paramount.

Can you start to choose your words more carefully? Instead of saying, "I can't do that," say "I'll try," "I'm learning that skill." Can you help build the world you want to live in with your words? Whether through kindness, creating laughter, comforting a friend, etc. your words can and will make a difference. I wish you the best of luck as you continue on your quest to be 1% better.

Reflection

Acknowledgements

From the bottom of my heart and with every cell in my body, I want to thank you for taking the time to read this book. It was the most fun I've ever had writing anything and I think that's in large part because I know it has the ability to make a difference in even one person's life. And if it can help one person feel better about themselves, then who knows where it can go from there.

I want to thank my friends and family who read the original 1% Better newsletter and gave me invaluable feedback and encouragement along the way. You helped fan the flame of the tiny torch I've carried for this idea for so long. This book wouldn't exist if it wasn't for you.

Finally, thank you to those of you who take the time to leave book reviews. As an independent author, the saying "reviews are like gold" is the truth. So, if you got anything out of this book, I'd be even more appreciative if you took the time to leave a review.

With immense gratitude,

Natalie

About the author

Natalie Saar is a journalist and writer based in Los Angeles, California. She has been telling stories to anyone who will listen since she was able to talk. After years of consuming true crime content, she developed a love of thrillers. Her stories feature everyday situations — but with an added twist. "Becoming 1% Better" is her first work of nonfiction, born out of a love of general curiosity about how we can better ourselves and treat those around us better.

Other works

Do What I Say

Finding Frogman

Attack

Stalker

You can find them all at nataliesaar.com/

www.ingramcontent.com/pod-product-compliance
Lightning Source LLC
Chambersburg PA
CBHW061724070526
44583CB00024B/3000